DAN ROMM

Things
Your Bridge
Teacher
Won't Tell
You

MASTER POINT PRESS | TORONTO

Master Point Press
331 Douglas Ave.
Toronto, Ontario, Canada
M5M 1H2
(416) 781-0351
Website: http://www.masterpointpress.com
Email: info@masterpointpress.com

Library and Archives Canada Cataloguing in Publication

Romm, Dan
    Things your bridge teacher won't tell you / written by Dan Romm.

ISBN 1-897106-13-0
ISBN 978-1-897106-13-6

    1. Contract bridge. I. Title.

GV1282.3.R54 2006   796.41'5   C2006-902110-4

Editor   Ray Lee
Cover and interior design   Olena S. Sullivan/New Mediatrix
Interior format and copyediting   Suzanne Hocking

Printed in Canada by Webcom Ltd.

1 2 3 4 5 6 7   10 09 08 07 06

Table of Contents

Foreword

I 've known Dan since we were both in our early twenties. In fact, he was one of my first regular partners when I was just beginning my bridge career. Even at that age, Dan showed a keen grasp of the game and had already earned a reputation as one of the rising stars in the Los Angeles area, before mysteriously vanishing from the duplicate scene. It was much later that I learned that he had kept up with bridge as a regular at the prestigious Cavendish West Club, playing against many of the game's stars.

In this book you will look inside the mind of an expert and learn valuable secrets that are indispensable for any player seeking to move to a higher level of expertise at either rubber or duplicate bridge. His illustrative hands are both educational and entertaining. His unique approach will expose you to a different way of looking at the game than you are probably used to and will broaden your perspective. I highly recommend that you make this book a cornerstone of your library and add Dan's potent tips to your bridge arsenal.

Paul Soloway
March, 2006

Introduction

You have probably never heard of me, especially if you play duplicate bridge exclusively. So why should you listen to me? The short answer is that I have more than held my own for over forty years against the world's best players. I played rubber bridge games in Los Angeles, which were available fourteen hours a day, seven days a week at the Cavendish West Club. Whenever the Cavendish needed a player to start a high-stakes game for any of the regular or visiting stars, I was the one they called. Such stars included Paul Soloway, Bob Hamman, Mike Lawrence, Zia Mahmood, Grant Baze, Billy Eisenberg, Fred Hamilton, Larry Cohen, Meyer Schliefer, Danny Kleinman, Rhoda Walsh and Gene Freed. Many celebrities also regularly visited the club including Lucille Ball, Don Adams, Omar Sharif, attorney Marcia Clark, boxing promoter Aileen Eaton, poker and gin rummy star Stu Ungar, entrepreneur Frank King, pianist Henry Rose, and songwriter George Bassman. Needless to say, there was always a good time to be had by all.

Over that time, I probably held as many or more bridge hands as any duplicate bridge player alive, mostly with or against the recognized stars of bridge, and I won more money in high-stakes games than anyone else at the Cavendish while playing against these same stars. By the time I was twenty-eight I had won or placed in several major tournaments (including the Blue Ribbon pairs and the National Life Master Men's pairs as well as several events at Bridge Week in Los Angeles, a.k.a. the 4th National). I then decided that, instead of pursuing more feathers to add to my cap (which would be an endless quest since I could never add enough to satisfy myself), I would leave the duplicate world for the greener pastures of rubber bridge.

Rubber bridge is an excellent experimental laboratory in which to put unconventional methods to the test to see if they work as well as or better than the accepted wisdom of the day. One gets to play with and against players of all skill levels and can study the thought processes of the weakest as well as the strongest. I spent the first three years of my rubber bridge career devoting ten hours a day to playing in the lowest stakes games so that I could afford to throw caution to the wind. I studied opponents' hesitations and gestures. I analyzed and documented the *results* of various approaches, including overcalling and balancing with three-card suits, deliberately overbidding or underbidding by one or more tricks, opening an unconventional 1NT, bidding 3NT with at most a partial stopper in suits bid by opponents, bidding game on hands of varying strength and/or distribution, preempting on weak and strong hands, making penalty doubles with anything or nothing, and opening hands with eight points. I compared the strengths of various conventions such as four-card vs. five-card majors, weak vs. intermediate vs. strong jump overcalls, penalty doubles vs. artificial doubles, weak two-bids vs. strong two-bids, various forms of Stayman, etc, etc. After each session I reviewed the effect of each action on both strong and weak players. My results steadily improved as I eliminated the ones that didn't work very well and incorporated the ones that did. As I moved into higher stakes games I did some fine-tuning. By the time I arrived at the highest stakes, my methods were so successful that I was winning enough to support myself through graduate school and beyond, with plenty left over.

My methods are, for the most part, original; they have been developed and tested heuristically. Many will conflict with what you have already read from experts. Although I have read some of the fashionable bridge books written by the recognized experts, I find that they often contain incomplete or faulty logic. Most bridge experts who write books are seeking to profit and the more books they sell the more money they make. They can't afford to wait until exceptional ideas occur to them; they must continually put out new material. Meanwhile I am under no such pressure. This bridge book, written at age 64, will be my first and last. I am not suggesting that there are no good ideas in such books, but you have to distinguish the good ones from the filler — the authors won't tell you. The more they write, the more filler they produce, hence the need for independent analysis.

To illustrate my point, let's look at a recent example taken from the mixed pairs at the Pittsburgh Nationals:

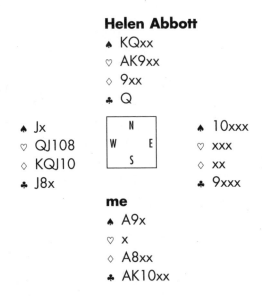

Helen Abbott
- ♠ KQxx
- ♡ AK9xx
- ◇ 9xx
- ♣ Q

♠ Jx	♠ 10xxx
♡ QJ108	♡ xxx
◇ KQJ10	◇ xx
♣ J8x	♣ 9xxx

me
- ♠ A9x
- ♡ x
- ◇ A8xx
- ♣ AK10xx

West	North	East	South
			1♣
pass	1♡	pass	1NT
pass	2◊¹	pass	3◊
pass	3NT	all pass	

1. New minor forcing.

Opening lead: ◊K

A nice feature of some Nationals is the production and distribution of a booklet containing deal analyses by various experts in addition to the usual hand records. On this deal, the booklet erroneously stated that making five seemed to be the maximum reasonable result. The experts failed to notice that, with correct technique, six always makes whenever West makes the routine continuation of the diamond queen after the king holds the first trick. (A heart shift will hold the contract to five, but this would be a very unusual play.) Do you see how you can make six?

Win the second diamond with the ace and lead a club to dummy's queen. Then make the somewhat unintuitive, but nevertheless correct, play of cashing the king and queen of spades from dummy. Doing so reveals the spade position when you next lead a spade to your ace. You will discover that the spades don't split and that dummy's fourth spade is wrongly positioned to pose a threat. You then cash the ace-king of clubs, discarding dummy's useless spade, getting the good news that the jack drops, and catch West in a heart-diamond squeeze as you play your remaining two clubs.

There are some recurrent themes interwoven throughout this book. I hope that, by way of repetition with variation, they will become ingrained in your psyche without your necessarily noticing. However, as in bridge, you will have to pay attention to nuances. Some messages may seem contradictory unless you notice the essential differences in each case. For instance, I advocate bidding immediately to a high level with some hands and waiting until you gather more information with somewhat similar hands. The key differences in each situation will be apparent if you attend to the crux of the matter under discussion. As I have limited experience with strong club systems and don't feel qualified to comment on them, the non-general bidding tips in this book are restricted to other types of systems, primarily 2/1.

As you read, always keep in mind that it is unwise to accept the ideas of purported experts in any field without an independent analysis. Even experts can miss things or get them wrong, including me. So before you either accept or reject my techniques, I suggest that you try them and analyze them for yourself.

DAN ROMM

Things
Your Bridge
Teacher
Won't Tell
You

CHAPTER 1

What Makes An Expert

THE 5 DIMENSIONS OF BRIDGE

Contrary to popular opinion, masterpoint totals are a poor indicator of expertise. To quote Paul Soloway, the current all-time masterpoint leader (who also happens to be a true expert), "masterpoints are an attendance record." A more useful statistic, akin to batting average as opposed to total hits, would be masterpoints per event played. Masterpoints notwithstanding, being an expert means being proficient in *all* of the following five components, each equally important: psychology, planning, technique, judgment and adaptability. We will consider each of them in detail.

Psychology: Table Presence and Awareness

The best table environment is one filled with friendliness, relaxation, humor, fun, fairness and non-defensiveness. Treat every tournament as if it were a social occasion. Put your best foot forward every time you meet new opponents. I am not suggesting that you must put up with rudeness by the opponents. It is okay to fight fire with fire, but don't initiate a confrontation. If opponents are trying to upset you, don't get mad, but do get even. Kibitzers are also fair game. If they are a distraction, don't hesitate to quiet them or even bar them; it is within your rights. I always bar kibitzers (even personal friends) whenever they lend excessive moral support to the opponents; you are entitled to a level playing field.

Play for the sheer love of the game. Solving the innumerable challenging problems that bridge presents should be reward enough. If you don't enjoy yourself when you play bridge, find another hobby. Sadly, most devotees of duplicate bridge are more interested in winning than in playing well. If your primary motivation is to boost your self-image by being highly regarded as a bridge player, you put so much pressure on yourself to play flawlessly that you can't relax and have fun. Ironically, your results will suffer as a result of the constant stress. Many players compulsively travel to major tournaments every week of their lives in order to enhance their status by ranking highly in the annual masterpoint listings. I worry about them. Imagine the mental and physical toll exacted by spending forty hours a week in an activity that you don't really enjoy.

The table presence of players who are only interested in winning often consists of a mixture of intense anxiety, rudeness to partners and opponents, superciliousness, condescension, sensitivity to criticism, being upset over and dwelling on bad results, looking for every edge from a director's rulings, being suspicious of an opponent's ethics, etc.

It is easy to one-up these players and take them off their game if you are so inclined. Merely contradict them or, better yet, politely belittle them. Be sure to point out any error they make at the table.

Assess the opposition; their skill level should determine your strategy. As will be pointed out many times in what follows, your approach should vary dramatically depending on whether your opponents are weak or strong. Be aggressive against weak players; be cautious against strong ones. I had an excellent opportunity to observe weak players in action at the beginning of my career. My brother Steve, Paul Soloway and Jerry Hallee ran a small duplicate bridge club in Santa Monica and I went there occasionally to help out when they were short-handed, either to direct the game or to play with anyone who needed a partner. Leo, a terrific guy but a hopeless player, was one of the regulars. He idolized us and thought we could do no wrong at the bridge table. Leo liked to show up without a partner just to play with one of us.

One time when I was playing with him we had the following auction:

Neither vul.

West	North	East	South
	Leo		Me
			1♠
pass	pass	dbl	pass
pass	2♠	pass	pass
dbl	all pass		

Leo certainly had his initial pass; he had two queens and a doubleton spade. Luckily for Leo and me, I had a pretty good hand and our opponents were weak. They defended badly and allowed me to make it. When I asked a beaming Leo why he had bid two spades, his answer should have been obvious to me. He replied simply, "I wanted the game bonus!"

Weak players do unfathomable things. The most befuddling example in my experience occurred when I was directing at the Santa Monica club. Near the end of the round everything was calm and peaceful at all tables, including table six where four of the weaker players were deep in concentration. As I was about to call the move, one of the foursome cried, "Director!" They were in a heated argument by the time I arrived. The deal had been completed and the score was about to be entered when it was discovered that North and South thought the contract was two hearts and East and West thought the contract was two diamonds! To this day I can't imagine how they had managed to play the entire deal before I was summoned.

You must be observant. Note all hesitations, facial expressions, mood swings and unusual gestures by the opponents (it is unethical to pay attention to those of your partner). Here are two examples:

One unusual gesture that you can't help but notice is how your opponent plays a card at his turn. Suppose you need to guess a card in a suit and when you lead the suit your opponent pulls out a card and carefully holds it instead of merely laying it on the table. If he hasn't been playing all of his cards in the same fashion, there is a nearly infallible inference to be drawn from this. What do you think it is? The answer is clear with a little reflection. If a non-expert opponent does this, he has the missing card! Why? Because the only way he would know that an important card is missing is if he were looking at it. If he held only unimportant cards in the suit, he would not play in an unusual manner.

In the late 1960s, I encountered Larry Weiss and Paul Soloway on the final day of the Blue Ribbon pairs. I was in 3NT, which depended on bringing in dummy's A-Q-J-10-x-x-x of diamonds. I held x-x in diamonds with no side entries to dummy. The first diamond finesse held, so I returned to my hand and led another diamond. Larry followed. After a little reflection, I played the ace, dropping Paul's king for all the matchpoints!

It was fun to see the reactions of the other three at the table. Larry was angry and muttered, "We got fixed by an impossible play." Paul frowned and said, "I have to hold my hand back." Tom looked stunned and just shook his head. To this day none of them knew how I figured out to play the ace and I never told them, until now. How did I do it? I merely trusted my table feel more than percentages, which you should also do whenever the signals are clear. Here is the complete deal:

Both vul.

Tom Lesser
♠ xx
♡ xx
◇ AQJ10xxx
♣ xx

Larry
♠ Kxx
♡ J109xx
◇ 92
♣ Kxx

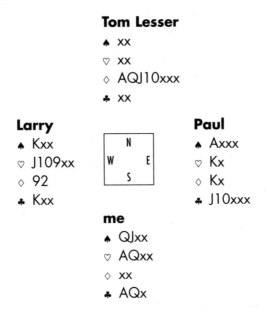

Paul
♠ Axxx
♡ Kx
◇ Kx
♣ J10xxx

me
♠ QJxx
♡ AQxx
◇ xx
♣ AQx

West	North	East	South
			1NT
pass	3NT	all pass	

Opening lead: ♡J

There were several clues which all suggested the play of the ace of diamonds the second time. First, when Paul played the king of hearts at Trick 1, Larry, not one to hide his emotions, looked pleased. I reasoned that he would be less serene had he held the king of diamonds. Second, on the first diamond, Larry carefully played the nine to give Paul the count, pushing it out and holding it out to make sure he noticed. Third, Paul played small with a self-satisfied expression on his face as if to say, "I just made an excellent play that will land us a top board." Which, in fact, he had. By this time I was so sure of the position that when Larry played the two on the second diamond, repeating the finesse was out of the question.

Naturally, the more you know about your opponent, the more likely it is that you will correctly read his mannerisms. Here is a deal I played in my early days at the Cavendish:

♠ QJx
♡ AQx
◇ AJxx
♣ KJx

☐

me
♠ Kx
♡ KJx
◇ K10xxx
♣ AQx

West	North	East	South
			1NT
pass	6NT	all pass	

Opening lead: ♠10

East wins with the ace of spades at Trick 1 and returns a spade. Clearly the contract hinges on successfully guessing the diamond suit. The difference between playing for a 2-2 split versus taking a finesse is a mere 2%. Can you do anything to improve your odds?

Lead the *jack* of hearts to the ace and then lead the *jack* of clubs from dummy! These plays give you an opportunity to observe how the opponents play their cards if they have no problem when an honor is led through them.[1]

Suppose one of them does something out of the ordinary. If it is West, cash the king of diamonds and lead the ten. If it is East, cash the ace of diamonds and lead the jack. In either case, take the finesse if the anomalous behavior is not repeated. On the actual deal, when I led the jack of clubs, East hesitated noticeably before following. When I next led the ace and jack of diamonds, he played low smoothly, so I successfully finessed his queen. (I cannot take sole credit for making this play. I was already familiar with the tactics used. Unfortunately, I don't remember my source.)

---

1.   Throughout this book an honor means ace, king, queen, jack or ten.

It is important always to stay alert. At all times you must anticipate declarer's plays so that you can prepare to make your own plays smoothly. If you hold a yarborough, look interested so as not to tip off your opponents. Actually, when playing with a weak partner, you should relish weak hands. Why? Because in any auction, the weak hand has more control than the strong one! The weak hand can slow down an over-ambitious partner and can always end the auction with a pass. In money rubber bridge, you must minimize losses, so how you handle weak hands is as important as how you handle strong ones. Here is an example of how you can capitalize on an opponent's loss of concentration:

Neither vul.

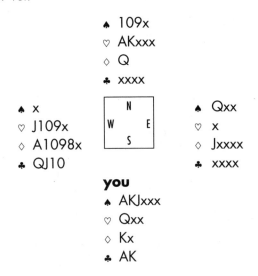

♠ 109x
♡ AKxxx
◇ Q
♣ xxxx

♠ x
♡ J109x
◇ A1098x
♣ QJ10

♠ Qxx
♡ x
◇ Jxxxx
♣ xxxx

you
♠ AKJxxx
♡ Qxx
◇ Kx
♣ AK

West	North	East	South
			2♣
pass	2♡	pass	2♠
pass	3♠	pass	4NT
pass	5◇	pass	6♠
all pass			

Opening lead: ♣Q

The contract depends on a successful guess of the trump queen. How can you improve your chances? Win the club lead with the ace; play the ace of spades and then the king — *of clubs*. This gives you a slim chance of catching West napping. He may have been expecting you to lead the king of spades next. If he pauses to consider his discard before following to the club, then this is a clue that he is out of spades and you should finesse his partner for the queen. On the actual deal you may get an additional bonus — West might discard a diamond before realizing that a club was led. If so, you can now lead to dummy's queen of diamonds immediately and make seven!

Maintain table presence even if you are in a seemingly hopeless contract, again so as not to tip off the opponents. During my salad days I frequented Al Okuneff's bridge club in Los Angeles before the Cavendish opened. In a team game with Al and Kai Larsen as my opponents and Bob Hamman as my partner, I arrived in 3NT on the following deal:

Neither vul.

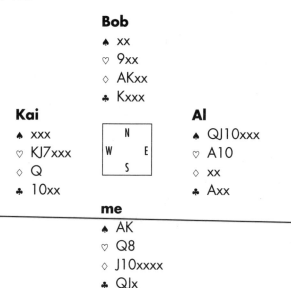

Bob
♠ xx
♡ 9xx
◇ AKxx
♣ Kxxx

Kai
♠ xxx
♡ KJ7xxx
◇ Q
♣ 10xx

Al
♠ QJ10xxx
♡ A10
◇ xx
♣ Axx

me
♠ AK
♡ Q8
◇ J10xxxx
♣ QJx

West	North	East	South
			1◇
2♡	3◇	3♠	3NT
pass	pass	dbl	all pass

Opening lead: low spade

With an air of approval when the dummy appeared, I nonchalantly won the spade ace and played a club to the king, won by Al. After some deliberation, he cashed the ace of hearts as I calmly followed low. He then went into a five-minute huddle and continued with a spade! What was his explanation to his partner? He couldn't believe that I would be so relaxed if I were wide open in one of the majors, so he played me for Ax of spades and Kx of hearts.

Needless to say, had I not maintained my table presence in light of such a dismal prospect of success, I would surely have been defeated. Much later, Hamman was widely quoted as saying that one should always bid 3NT when there is any chance, no matter how slight, of making it. I like to believe that this deal was the beginning of his insight.

Being a good partner

Several otherwise excellent players fall out of expert status by ignoring this extremely important aspect of the game. If your partner makes an error (as we all do occasionally, even the best), note it on your card for discussion after the session, preferably over a beer. *Do not* even so much as mention it at the table. If your partner voluntarily apologizes, smile sweetly and say, "No problem." One bad board will not cost you an event, but acting like a wounded animal will cost you many. Bridge is a partnership game and if you upset your partner, causing him to blow the next board too (as usually happens), your entire session will unravel. The urge to show off by verbally pointing out your partner's errors while at the table and in front of the opponents is an indication of low self-confidence. Many an event has been lost in this way. Besides, you may end up with egg on your face when you discover that your analysis was faulty — especially if the error turns out to be yours!

My main avenue for success in money rubber bridge has been to treat the weaker players with respect. In case you don't know, the key to money bridge is to get good results with weak partners. Being a hand hog is especially risky. Just because someone is a weak bridge player doesn't mean that he is stupid! Most weak players in high-stakes rubber bridge games are wealthy and are there for recreational enjoyment. They can well afford to lose. If you disrespect them, they will notice and may get even just to spite you. Here is a case in point:

One of the regulars in our game was Doctor Ben, a loveable dentist who was addicted to bridge and affluent enough to lose graciously. He particularly enjoyed playing with me and when I was his partner he would play his heart out (not for his sake, but for mine). Although he was a competent bidder, he had no innate card sense, so that his results usually did not match his desire. Nevertheless, I always let him play the deals that were rightfully his to play. If he went down in a cold contract, I said, "Nice try." If he managed to cash his nine off the top in 3NT, I said, "Way to go!"

One day a pro, not knowing the players, joined our game. It didn't take him long to recognize Ben's deficiencies. Although he was benefiting from Ben's mistakes when playing against him, he decided that he couldn't afford to let Ben make the same mistakes when he was his partner. So, surreptitiously (he thought), he started playing the infamous two-way transfers. For those of you unfamiliar with this well-known rubber bridge hand-hogging technique, it merely means that while your partner, holding a five-card major, dutifully transfers when *you* open 1NT, you jump to three of your major when *he* opens 1NT. The upshot is that in both cases you get to be declarer.

Well, it worked all right for a while and the pro was happily building up his winnings. But, unbeknownst to the pro, Ben was noticing what was going on and was not pleased. On the last rubber that they played together that evening Ben, intentionally I'm sure, made four uncharacteristically horrendous bids in four deals and misplayed them even worse than usual, resulting in four large numbers for the opponents. When the damage was logged, the pro had lost all his winnings and then some! That was the last time this pro played in our game.

Deception

Always bid aggressively, even more so against weak opponents. When playing weak opposition in money bridge, you must constantly apply pressure. Take chances — deceptively light overcalls and preempts are essential. Although they occasionally backfire, they are relatively safe and will yield large dividends in the long run. Why? Because the opponents have to do three things right to punish you and it is unlikely that weak players will succeed at all three: (1) one of them has to double rather than taking the push, something he will be reluctant to do if he thinks you're an expert declarer; (2) the doubler's partner has to sit, again a distasteful option to him for the same reason; (3) they *both* have to defend well, which is even harder for them to do when they are playing you for a better hand than you have.

Deception is also effective against strong players (but you need to be more cautious). At money rubber bridge against Larry Weiss, a staunch advocate of four-card majors, and Fran Tsacnaris, an excellent rubber bridge player, I picked up

♠ KQJ109xx ♡ AKQxx ◇ — ♣ x

Both sides were vulnerable. After two passes, RHO (Weiss) opened one heart. What do you bid? I chose the deceptive bid — pass. I figured the auction wouldn't die and I had the boss suit so I could wait to see how the auction would develop. Lo and behold, Fran (who never opened without full values) bid four hearts, which I doubled and she promptly redoubled. Here is the complete deal:

Both vul.

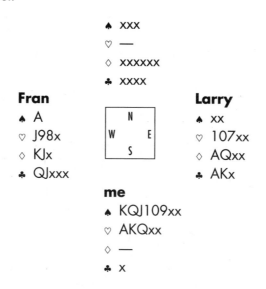

♠ xxx
♡ —
◇ xxxxxx
♣ xxxx

Fran
♠ A
♡ J98x
◇ KJx
♣ QJxxx

Larry
♠ xx
♡ 107xx
◇ AQxx
♣ AKx

me
♠ KQJ109xx
♡ AKQxx
◇ —
♣ x

West	North	East	South
pass	pass	1♡	pass*
4♡	pass	pass	dbl
redbl	all pass		

Opening lead: ♠K

I led the spade king, which lost to dummy's ace. As expected, dummy tabled four trumps. Larry now made the disastrous mistake of thinking one round of trumps was safe! After the smoke cleared, our side had collected a cool 4000. My partner was ecstatic to get this result with his hand and the game promptly ended amid numerous vociferous recriminations between Fran and Larry.

A good opportunity for deception arises after partner opens with a weak two-bid. Here are two tips to keep in mind:

Furthering any preempt either to keep opponents out of game or slam, or to push them into one that you can beat, quite often has the opposite effect. This is especially true when the opponents are not playing Lebensohl. Don't automatically raise a weak two-bid merely because you have trump support. First ask yourself the key question, "Do I want the opponents in or out of the auction?"

Most players automatically raise in order to keep the opponents out. The right approach is to consider how the subsequent bidding is likely to go and then make your most deceptive bid. Here is an example. You hold:

♠ Axx   ♡ Jxx   ◊ QJ10x   ♣ KQx

Both vul.

West	North	East	South
pass	2♡	pass	?

Many players misguidedly bid three hearts with this hand to keep opponents from finding their spade fit. Pass is clearly best. For one thing, West may very well have too little to bid over two hearts. If so, you will be delighted to declare at the two-level if that's all you can make. For another, on this deal you *want* the opponents to discover their spade fit. Knowing they have a fit may induce them, over your next round bid of three hearts, to carry on to three spades, which you would happily double at matchpoints since they are unlikely to make it. Moreover, even if they don't take the push, you are no worse off than if you had bid three hearts directly.

If your RHO doubles your partner's weak two-spade bid and you hold a singleton or void in spades with lots of defense on the outside (a hand with which you are eagerly waiting to double them when they bid) don't pass — redouble! Unless your opponents are a well-seasoned partnership and have an agreement that a pass of a redouble in this situation is for penalties, redoubling ensures that you get your wish to defend.

You succeed by deception since the doubler won't think that his partner's pass could be for penalties, and will run. On the other hand, passing runs the risk that the doubler's partner will convert his partner's takeout double to a penalty double with a spade stack. This is a likely possibility since the one who doubled is usually short in spades, as are you. You may still make, but then again you may not, whereas you are sure of a large profit if you defend.

Along the same lines, here is a deal that came up in the open pairs at the Seattle regional. I was playing with Bob Hitchens for the first time and our opponents were Patsy Esfeld and Sharon Miller. I picked up:

♠ AK9xx   ♡ x   ◇ AKxx   ♣ xxx

Neither vul.

West	North	East	South
			1♠
2♡	pass	pass	dbl
redbl	pass	pass	?

You ask East what redouble means and she says partner has a good hand and thinks she can make. What do you bid with no relevant partnership agreement other than negative doubles?

Partner may have had a penalty pass, in which case you should pass if you trust your partner (and I certainly trusted Bob), since he could have pulled the redouble if his pass was shaky. But then, your partner didn't ask what the redouble meant and he might have thought it was for rescue (before he heard East pass).

I decided to pass for three reasons. First, my shortness in hearts made it more likely that partner's pass was for penalties than from weakness. Second, I had a good defensive hand. Third, Patsy may have realized that her side was in trouble anywhere and she is a good enough player to make an anti-system bid deceptively and deliberately in order to scare us from sitting.

It turns out that Patsy did indeed have a good hand, in fact a very good hand; she certainly didn't want partner to run. It also turns out that Bob did indeed think that the redouble was for takeout and, although he did have heart length, his pass was from weakness. Here is the complete deal:

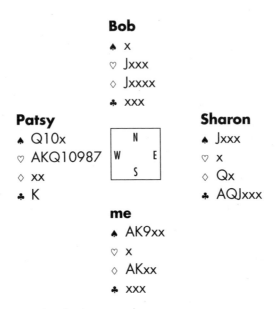

Bob
- ♠ x
- ♡ Jxxx
- ◊ Jxxxx
- ♣ xxx

Patsy
- ♠ Q10x
- ♡ AKQ10987
- ◊ xx
- ♣ K

Sharon
- ♠ Jxxx
- ♡ x
- ◊ Qx
- ♣ AQJxxx

me
- ♠ AK9xx
- ♡ x
- ◊ AKxx
- ♣ xxx

Opening lead: low spade

As luck would have it, two hearts went down one. Bob led his singleton spade. I cashed the ♠A-K and led the nine to request a diamond return. Bob ruffed and carefully returned his fourth-best diamond, whereupon I cashed the ◊A-K and returned a spade, uppercutting West for down one and +200 for us.[1]

Deception is also important as declarer or defender. Clever falsecarding is imperative on most deals. Needless to say, the less the opponents can infer about your hand from your plays, the better.

---

1. We had bad luck on a later deal, which cost us the event. I briefly want to discuss that deal, although it is off the subject, because I think the current bridge rule that covers it is misguided. Midway through the last session, we received a board with fourteen cards in Bob's hand and twelve in mine.

Unfortunately, neither Bob nor I had counted our cards before he bid. We were given an average minus on the board, whereas had we been given the right hands we would have easily bid and made game, which would have sufficed for a win.

My point is this. True, the case could be made that our side was a tad remiss. But no one should have to anticipate a fouled board midway through the session. After all, how can a card magically transform itself from the North to the South side of a board? Obviously, the main culprits were the pairs who had passed the board to us. For all practical purposes, we were merely innocent victims. I believe that a better way to handle this situation is, after round one, to give the guilty parties at the other table an average minus and the pairs at our table an average.

With two equally good lines of play available, choose the one most likely to confuse the opponents. Here are three examples:

This deal occurred in a star-studded pairs competition at Al Okuneff's club:

E-W vul.

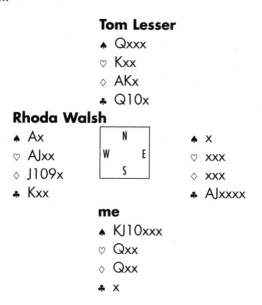

Tom Lesser
- ♠ Qxxx
- ♡ Kxx
- ♢ AKx
- ♣ Q10x

Rhoda Walsh
- ♠ Ax
- ♡ AJxx
- ♢ J109x
- ♣ Kxx

- ♠ x
- ♡ xxx
- ♢ xxx
- ♣ AJxxxx

me
- ♠ KJ10xxx
- ♡ Qxx
- ♢ Qxx
- ♣ x

West	North	East	South
			2♠
dbl	4♠	all pass	

Opening lead: ♢J

How do you proceed? It appears that you must lose one spade, two hearts and one club unless you find either opponent with ace doubleton (or singleton) of hearts, highly unlikely on the bidding. There is also a slim chance that you can negotiate a successful elimination play, but this would require a defensive slip. There is, however, a deceptive play available that greatly increases your odds: win the diamond in your hand with the queen and lead a low heart at Trick 2!

This line presents West with an unsolvable dilemma. If you hold a singleton heart and Jxx of clubs, she must rise with her ace of hearts to beat you (unless there is an unlikely ruff available). However, if she does so on the actual deal, you will make. Furthermore, she probably will go up with the ace (as did Rhoda), since your play seems somewhat unusual holding Q-x-x of hearts.

This deal illustrates another important point when it comes to deception: play so as to give the opponents the least chance of unmasking your ploy. If you pull trumps before leading up to the king of hearts, you give East a chance to make a revealing discard. Also, leading a heart immediately at Trick 2 creates a stronger illusion of a singleton than waiting would.

Playing matchpoints, I encountered the following deal:

Neither vul.

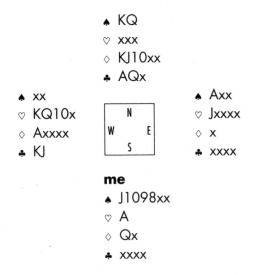

West	North	East	South
1◊	1NT	pass	2♠
all pass			

Opening lead: ♡K

You infer from the opening lead that West probably holds K-Q-10 of hearts, either A-x-x-x or A-x-x-x-x of diamonds, and either the ace of spades or the king of clubs for his opening bid. How do you proceed?

Although it seems that leading trumps is right in order to circumvent a diamond ruff, deception has a better chance of succeeding. Lead a low diamond at Trick 2! You will probably make five whenever East holds the spade ace and a singleton diamond, whereas if you lead a trump, you will be held to four. True, the recommended play will be wrong whenever East is void in diamonds and also holds the ace of spades, but this is less likely than a singleton or doubleton. Indeed, the recommended play costs nothing if East has a doubleton. With the recommended play, West has to rise with the ace of diamonds (instead of ducking) and return one (instead of trying to cash a second heart). If he doesn't, then you can safely start trumps, having stripped East of his singleton diamond. On the other hand, if you lead a trump at Trick 2, East will have no problem winning with the ace and returning a diamond for a ruff.

Here is a simple falsecarding rule involving the nine of trumps that I have derived from personal experience. If you don't have a trump trick by brute force, i.e. J-10-9-x, whenever giving partner a count in trumps is irrelevant and it is unnecessary to preserve a spot card for an overruff, *always* play the nine on the first round. Although there may exist a deal on which this is the wrong play, I have never encountered it and, in fact, I can't even think one up.

The deceptive effect of this play is powerful indeed. Here are two well-known examples that, without my rule as an umbrella, were heretofore considered as two unrelated situations:

Consider these two possible positions where East is declarer in four spades:

POSITION 1

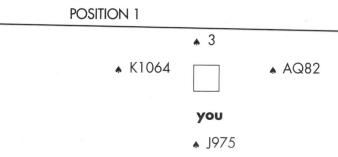

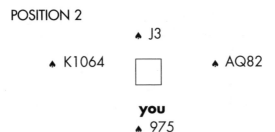

♠ J3

♠ K1064   ♠ AQ82

you
♠ 975

In both cases, declarer begins correctly by cashing the ace. Equally correct, however, according to the rule, is to drop the nine! If you don't, declarer will continue with the queen to protect against your holding of four to the jack and will make his contract. If you drop the nine instead, declarer will lead low towards dummy's king at Trick 2 to protect against J-7-5-3 in North's hand (unless he knows that you know my rule!) and encounter a rude shock when you follow with a low spade!

If you hold Hand 1, he will have to play dummy's ten; if you hold Hand 2, he will have to play dummy's king. Quite a dilemma. If he decides to play the ten and you hold Hand 2, he will have a hard time explaining how he lost a trump trick!

Suppose you are defending as South on the following deal with spades as trumps:

dummy
♠ A72

you
♠ 1094

Declarer, West, leads the queen of spades and plays the two from dummy, partner playing the five. According to the rule, you play the nine. Clearly, the play of the nine can't cost. Do you see how it can gain? Here is the rest of the spade suit:

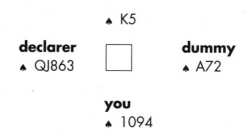

♠ K5

declarer
♠ QJ863

dummy
♠ A72

you
♠ 1094

If you play the four, declarer has no choice other than continuing with a low spade, capturing partner's king and losing no trump tricks. But if you play the nine, declarer may well play you for a doubleton 109 and continue with the queen.

It's true that partner could have covered the queen the first time, but this is the wrong play since it is inferior to ducking whenever you have the much more likely holding of 10-x-x without the nine. Suppose this is the situation:

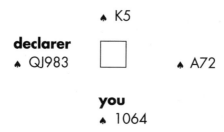

♠ K5

declarer
♠ QJ983

♠ A72

you
♠ 1064

If partner covers the queen, declarer will win with the ace and probably finesse your ten. (An expert West playing against an expert North will be wary of North holding doubleton K-10, but since singleton king is more likely, he should finesse against the ten anyway.) If partner ducks, however, declarer again has a choice. He can play you for 10-x-x and partner for K-x and continue with a low heart, which happens to work this time, or he can play you for 10-x and partner for K-x-x and continue with the queen, which fails. He will choose the losing play of the queen more often than not since most players make the wrong play of covering the queen with K-x.

Concealment is also an important part of deception. With a choice of plays, choose the less revealing one. This is an obvious example, but its basic principle is often neglected. At matchpoints, you hold:

E-W vul.

♠ Axx
♥ AK
♦ J10xx
♣ A10xx

[ ]

you
♠ KQJ10xxxx
♥ xxx
♦ —
♣ Qx

West	North	East	South
			4♠
pass	6♠	all pass	

Opening lead: ♥J

Clearly you want to ruff a heart, so you cash the ♥A-K. How do you proceed? You should routinely take the least revealing approach. Accordingly, you lead a trump to your hand, ruff a heart with the ace of trumps and return to your hand with a trump. *Do not* ruff a diamond! Doing so will give the opponents knowledge about your distribution to which they are not entitled and will make it much easier for them to find the right discards when you run trumps.

I conclude this section with one of the finest examples of deception that I have ever seen. The great Victor Mitchell made this deservedly famous play and, although you may have already seen it, it is certainly worth another look:

Neither vul.

```
                    ♠ xx
                    ♡ AKJx
                    ◊ xx
                    ♣ QJ9xx
   ♠ K10xxx                        ♠ Jxx
   ♡ xxx          ┌─────────┐      ♡ xxxx
   ◊ AQx          │ N       │      ◊ KJxx
   ♣ Kx           │ W     E │      ♣ xx
                  │    S    │
                  └─────────┘
```

Mitchell
- ♠ AQx
- ♡ Qx
- ◊ xxxx
- ♣ A10xx

West	North	East	South
	1♣	pass	2NT
pass	3NT	all pass	

Opening lead: low spade

When the jack of spades came up on his right, Mitchell promptly won — with the ace, not the queen. He then led a low heart to dummy and took a club finesse. Needless to say, West failed to find the killing diamond switch when he won with the king of clubs. He continued with a low spade, expecting to find partner with the spade queen and Mitchell claimed ten tricks.

Note that a diamond switch by West would have been obvious had Mitchell won the first spade with the queen, since East would have won the first trick with the ace of spades had he held it.

Mental Toughness

To excel in any form of competition, you need to have, or learn to have, a thick skin. This holds especially true for bridge, a mental sport where a lapse in concentration can be fatal. Don't obsess over an error. Even the best players make boneheaded plays occasionally. To quote Michael Rosenberg, "Nobody's any good at this game; the top players are just less bad than the rest." Here are two examples taken from actual high-stakes money-bridge situations involving two of the game's biggest names. These examples are not included to denigrate great players, who make far fewer errors than most, but to illustrate that we are all human.

One of the game's recognized superstars and a prolific author of popular bridge books was in a vulnerable grand slam. (No, it wasn't Eddie Kantar.) He had played the deal well and had managed to come down to a two-card end position. He held the ace and deuce of trumps and there was only one other outstanding trump, known to be in LHO's hand. In order to make, he had to successfully ruff a card from dummy with his deuce without being overruffed. With a choice of two suits to lead from dummy, what did this great player do? He led the only card outstanding in the club suit (the thirteenth)! Since everybody was out of clubs, he went down, whereas his LHO would have had to follow suit if the other card had been led from dummy.

Another of the game's greatest stars and a winner of many world championships was in a vulnerable slam. (If you guessed Bob Hamman, you are wrong again.) After losing the first trick and winning the second, he went into deep thought. He ultimately led the five of diamonds towards dummy's A-x-x and when the six appeared on his left, he promptly played low. In his eagerness to rectify the count for a possible squeeze, he forgot that he had lost the first trick, thereby going down in a slam that actually had twelve tricks off the top! Incidentally, I never saw either of these two players in a money game again.

It is important not to appear upset over a bad result. Instead, remain calm in order to create the impression that you are good enough to overcome one disaster easily on your way to winning. The truth is that even four or five bad results will rarely undo you if the rest of your game is solid. John Swanson (a former representative of the USA in world team championships) and I were running late on our way to a sectional just outside of Los Angeles. When we finally arrived, the co-directors told us that they had been filling in for us and had played six disastrous boards, all bottoms, and would just continue playing if we wanted them to. Well, having nothing else to do, we took over from there. They were right; we got only two matchpoints in the six boards they played. Nevertheless, we won the event by a full board!

When you are having a run of bad cards, don't complain; look at it as an opportunity to practice your defense, or find some other way to enjoy yourself despite your temporary misfortune. In a money rubber bridge game, minimizing losses is just as important as maximizing gains and you can't do that if you are brooding over your bad luck. Luck is part of the game. In any duplicate event there are always at least a dozen or so pairs that are capable of winning. Which of them actually does win is the one with the most luck.

Luck comes in many forms. One form is when the deals are "your kind of deals". If you are proficient at declarer play, you will often seem to be 'lucky' as declarer; if you are proficient at opening leads, you will often seem to be 'lucky' on lead; if you are proficient at knowing when to double, your opponents will seem to step out of line more often. An obvious corollary is that the more complete your game is, the 'luckier' you will be.

Another kind of luck is when you have many opportunities to utilize your specific conventions, especially the ones that don't usually come up, and the opponents have few opportunities to use theirs. There are sessions in which you have a slim chance to win unless you play a weak notrump or a strong club. There are also sessions in which you get 'fixed' often by the opponents' conventions.

The most usual form of luck is when the opponents make many mistakes against you. Mike Dorn Wiss and I once won a regional open pairs event because, on the last board, the opponents bid a slam off two cashing aces *after* they had used Blackwood!

At duplicate, never be intimidated by reputation (the expert's biggest edge). Even the greats can't overcome correct bidding and play by you. When we were just embarking on our bridge careers, Paul Ivaska and I sat down against two of the game's biggest stars, Bobby Wolff and Jim Jacoby, in a regional open pairs. This was the deal:

N-S vul.

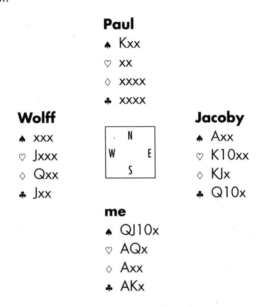

Paul
- ♠ Kxx
- ♡ xx
- ♢ xxxx
- ♣ xxxx

Wolff
- ♠ xxx
- ♡ Jxxx
- ♢ Qxx
- ♣ Jxx

Jacoby
- ♠ Axx
- ♡ K10xx
- ♢ KJx
- ♣ Q10x

me
- ♠ QJ10x
- ♡ AQx
- ♢ Axx
- ♣ AKx

West	North	East	South
	pass	1♢	dbl
1♡	pass	2♡	dbl
all pass			

Opening lead: low spade

Wolff, figuring we were a couple of young palookas who could easily be intimidated, bid a booming one heart with the West hand. As we collected our 300, the contempt that Jacoby expressed for his partner's bid was still ringing in our ears as we made our way to the next table.

You, on the other hand, *should* try to intimidate your opponents. Do it with class by exuding confidence, not with surliness or disrespect (in fact, these are signs of a lack of confidence). At the Cavendish, I fostered a reputation as a 'good card holder' by openly acknowledging my luck when I held good hands and never voicing displeasure when I held bad ones. This had an intimidating effect on my opponents, who expected me to win and became increasingly reluctant to double me. In addition, regular attendees attributed my consistent winning to luck rather than skill so that they continued to seek me out when choosing games in which to play.

Planning

The single most important purely technical skill is learning how to approach the play and defense of a deal. As you have undoubtedly heard on numerous occasions, you must begin this process at Trick 1. If you adopt the wrong starting approach, all the subsequent counting and logic will usually not suffice to bail you out. Here are two examples:

This wild deal occurred in a high stakes rubber bridge game at the Cavendish against Bill Sides and Richard Rogers:

Both vul.

Larry Cohen
♠ AKJ10xxx
♡ —
◊ Axx
♣ KQx

me
♠ —
♡ xxx
◊ xxx
♣ AJ98xxx

West	North	East	South
			3♣
dbl	6♣	pass	pass
6♡	6♠	dbl	7♣
all pass			

Opening lead: ◊K

As the opening lead was tabled, I heard the announcement that there were two minutes to closing time. How do you analyze the deal and how do you proceed? Be forewarned — if you don't make the right play at Trick 2 you will be unable to recover!

While you are thinking, I will tell you that one of the kibitzers, Danny Kleinman (an excellent writer), drafted an article about the deal that very night. It included all possible spade distributions, the odds of each, the best play in each situation, and a conclusion. When he showed it to me the following afternoon and asked for feedback, I responded that, although his analysis was thorough and accurate, I had used a more practical approach. For one thing, there wasn't nearly enough time available to me to go through such a lengthy analysis. More importantly, such an analysis was both unnecessary and irrelevant. The right play is immediately apparent if you correctly approach the deal. The first step is to realize that if trumps are 3-0, the contract is unmakeable, provided that the double of six spades wasn't totally crazy. If they are 2-1, however, as they must be to have any chance, there is a line of play (and as it turns out, the only one) that completely guarantees the contract.

The solution? After winning the ace of diamonds, ruff a low spade with the jack of trumps, lead a club to dummy (luckily everybody follows), ruff another spade with the ace of trumps, lead a club to dummy and play on spades (ruffing out the queen in the process). This yields four spades, the diamond ace, a heart ruff in dummy and seven club tricks from hand for thirteen in all. Incidentally, had you carelessly ruffed the first spade low, West would have overruffed with the ♣10.

This second example is based on a deal from Steve Becker's syndicated newspaper column "Contract Bridge", but I have added some material of my own. You are South in six diamonds:

```
            ♠ Kx
            ♡ Ax
            ◊ Jxxx
            ♣ AKJ10x

Opening lead: ♡J    [ ]
                    you
            ♠ Ax
            ♡ Kx
            ◊ AQ8xxx
            ♣ xxx
```

There are two possible losers, the trump king and the club queen. How do you play the deal? A good player will realize that the best approach is to guard against a singleton king of trumps offside by first stripping out the majors and then playing the ace of diamonds. There is no point in taking the diamond finesse. If East holds the K-x of trumps, he can be thrown in and forced to either lead a club or offer a sluff and ruff. On the other hand, if West holds the guarded king of diamonds, you can still fall back on the club finesse. A true expert will carry the logic a step further. You can increase your chances of success by roughly 6%. Do you see how?

After cashing your major-suit winners, *lead the jack* of diamonds toward your ace. If East plays low, go up with the ace to try to catch the singleton king offside as planned. If East shows out, merely pass the jack. This play costs nothing, but it gains whenever West is void in diamonds. In this case East, holding K-10-9, will cover your jack. As a result, he will still be endplayed when you cash the queen and exit. If you had merely led a low diamond to your ace, East would be able to exit safely with his third trump.

A good planner must be flexible. He will begin with the best approach, but will make necessary modifications as the play unfolds. I have already remarked about the danger of hasty play at Trick 1, so I won't elaborate further other than to state that if you have a choice of winning the opening lead in either hand, don't thoughtlessly make the 'natural-looking' play before taking stock of your entries. For instance, it frequently happens that in a suit contract, dummy has K-x-x of the led suit opposite A-x in your hand. Don't win the opening lead with the ace before planning your entire sequence of plays. It may well be right to make the 'unnatural' play of winning the first trick with the king in order to preserve an entry to your hand.

As important as planning the play is, planning the bidding is even more so! The best bidders plan their entire sequence of bids rather than focusing on the bid at hand. They realize that one bid will frequently not suffice to adequately describe their hands, so they don't try to make one bid do too much. They also realize that on many deals it is not necessary, and sometimes even foolhardy, to try to describe their hands. Instead, they adopt a plan of deception.

Lesser bidders meanwhile make the bid that conforms to their system at each turn. They mistakenly believe that the better they accomplish this, the better they bid. Consequently, they refuse ever to make a bid that violates their system. The folly of this approach cannot be overstated.

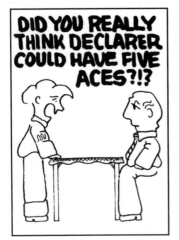

Technique (Counting and Drawing Inferences)

Although most players believe that the hallmark of an expert is counting suits, I consider this one of the least important tools in the expert's kit. If you don't agree, you are probably spending far too much time and mental energy counting suits and not nearly enough on the other aspects of good bridge, such as planning, drawing inferences, deception and paying attention to details, none of which requires counting as a prerequisite.

Most hands are not worth counting; logic will give you all the information you need. Rather than immediately beginning a count of every suit, pay attention to each trick and note when someone shows out. You can then reconstruct count later if and when it is necessary. Usually the mere fact that an opponent is short in one or more suits will tip you off on how to play the other suits without needlessly ascertaining the exact count. On defense, I recommend that the only suit you begin counting immediately on every deal is trumps. This is essential in order to determine whether or not tapping declarer is fruitless, or whether or not offering a sluff and ruff is the right defense.

You must learn to watch all spot cards carefully. This is the most important detail of all. Not knowing that dummy's eight is high can be quite embarrassing! If you are attempting a squeeze, watching spots is safer and often easier than counting. For instance, suppose you have the eight of diamonds in the dummy and the ace, king and queen of diamonds have already been played. As you are running a long suit from your hand, the opponents start pitching diamonds. There are two methods you can use to determine if your eight becomes high. One way is to count diamonds (but this may not suffice unless all thirteen diamonds are accounted for). Another is to make a mental note that there are three outstanding diamonds higher than the eight (in this case, the jack, ten and nine). Then, reduce this number by one whenever one of those three is discarded. When the count reaches zero, you know your eight is good! This method is easiest since it is simpler to count to three than to count to thirteen.

Counting points is another matter, and you should begin a tentative point count of partner's hand every time an opponent has shown a specific range. For instance, if RHO has opened a 15-17 point 1NT, tentatively put him on 16. This will enable you to determine partner's points to within a jack. (It is easiest to keep track of partner's points since he usually has far fewer than the 1NT opener.) Then, if RHO becomes declarer, defend on the basis that partner holds a card or cards that are within his known range.

It is essential to draw inferences from what partner and opponents do. Some are clear and some are subtle. Equally important, but frequently overlooked, are the inferences that can be drawn from what your partner or an opponent *doesn't* do. There is usually more than one choice of play or bid in any given situation. You must always ask yourself why partner or an opponent chose this particular play or made this particular bid rather than another one at this particular point in the deal. Here is an example, taken from Becker's syndicated newspaper column, "Contract Bridge", of an inference drawn from what a defender *doesn't* do:

Both vul.

```
            ♠ AQx
            ♡ xxxx
            ◊ QJx
            ♣ Axx

            ┌─────┐
            │     │
            └─────┘

            you
            ♠ xx
            ♡ AKJx
            ◊ A108x
            ♣ xxx
```

West	North	East	South
	1♣	pass	1♡
pass	2♡	pass	4♡
all pass			

Opening lead: ♣Q

You duck the first club and win the continuation, East dropping the king. You now lead a low trump to the king and follow with a spade to dummy's queen, losing to the king. Back comes a low club to West's ten and a spade is led to dummy's ace. Having lost three tricks, you take the mandatory diamond finesse and the queen holds, as does the jack. On the jack, West drops the nine. Clearly it is now time to tackle trumps and when you lead one from the dummy, East follows low. Now what?

Although the percentages favor finessing the queen, it is clearly wrong to do so on this deal. You can infer that East did not start with Q-x-x of trumps since if he did, he would have *covered the jack of diamonds* to guarantee a set! So, when he doesn't, your only hope is to play West for Qx of trumps. Here is the complete deal:

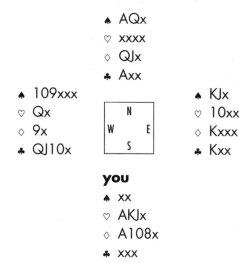

Here is another instance of drawing bidding inferences from what isn't done as well as from what is, this time during the auction. Suppose your opponent opens two hearts and partner bids three spades. Obviously he has length in spades, but how strong is he? There are at least six bidding sequences at his disposal to show spade length: two spades, three spades, four spades, double followed by a spade bid, double followed by a jump in spades or a cuebid followed by a spade bid. You and partner should discuss these various sequences, decide their meanings, and consider their nuances. With this many options, I recommend that at least one of them should be reserved for a weak hand. What do you prefer with A-K-Q-J-x-x and out (clearly you must be able to make some bid with this hand)? With A-J-10-9-x-x-x? With Q-J-9-x-x-x-x? With six spades and 20 points? Even without an agreement, if you ask yourself why partner selected his particular bid rather than another, you should be able to infer his strength fairly closely.

You can draw inferences from what partner doesn't hold as well as from what he doesn't bid. The following deal occurred at the Cavendish against Harold Guiver and Jim Kauder while I was playing with a stranger. My partner and I were playing regular old quantitative Blackwood with no queen-asking bid:

♠ AKJ10xx   ♡ QJx   ◇ x   ♣ KQJ

Both vul.

West	North	East	South
	2NT	pass	3♡
pass	3♠	pass	4♣
pass	4◇	pass	4NT
pass	5♠	pass	?

Clearly a grand slam depends on whether or not partner holds the spade queen, but how can you find out whether or not he does? Bid 5NT! You and partner hold either 37 or 38 points between you, leaving only 2 or 3 points outstanding. If partner is missing a king, then he must have the queen of spades. If he is not missing a king then he is missing either the queen of spades or the queen of diamonds. Since you can't know which, it is best to settle for a small slam.

On the actual deal, partner hesitated slightly (only he knows why) and responded six diamonds (one king), whereupon I bid 7NT, knowing he must have the spade queen. When he claimed his thirteen tricks off the top, Harold said accusingly, "You would never have bid seven off a king without the hesitation!" I responded, "How could I know why he was hesitating? I assumed he was thinking about what to have for lunch tomorrow." When I then explained my reasoning, Harold saw the light and capitulated.

You must also draw inferences from your partner's plays and the bidding as a *defender*. If you don't, partnership confidence will quickly erode. Here is an obvious example of a commonplace inference that you can draw from your partner, one that is missed surprisingly often by non-experts. Against a slam in a suit, you lead the king from A-K-10-8 and dummy tables Q-J-9-7-6. Partner plays the three and declarer the four. Should you continue? On the one hand, it seems unlikely that the opponents would bid a slam off two cashing tricks. But if you trust partner's carding, the ace must cash! The key question to ask is, who has the two of spades? If declarer has it, your ace will obviously cash. If partner has it, he has started an echo so he has a doubleton and, once again, your ace will cash.

Here is a subtler example in which you must draw inferences from both the bidding and the play. Playing in a team match at a Seattle regional with Mike Wilson as my partner, I held the following hand:

N-S vul.

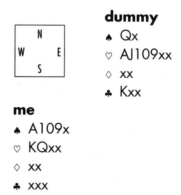

dummy
- ♠ Qx
- ♡ AJ109xx
- ◇ xx
- ♣ Kxx

me
- ♠ A109x
- ♡ KQxx
- ◇ xx
- ♣ xxx

West	North	East	South
1◇	pass	1♡	pass
3◇	pass	3♡	pass
3NT	all pass		

Opening lead: ♠2

Declarer plays a low spade from dummy at Trick 1. How do you defend? It appears that the automatic play at Trick 1 is to play the nine so as to hold declarer to only one spade trick instead of two in the event that he started with K-x-x. But, as I will repeat many times in this book, there are no automatic plays in bridge. You must always factor in the particulars of any given deal and be ready to modify your play accordingly. Logic, not automatic play, is the essence of good bridge.

The only successful defense is to win with the ace of spades at Trick 1! Furthermore, this play becomes obvious if you pay attention to the following relevant clues. The lead of the two of spades, coupled with West's failure to bid one spade over one heart, marks Mike with exactly four spades and declarer with exactly three. West must have at least six diamonds for his three diamond bid. West's failure to bid four hearts over three along with his weak spade holding suggests at most one heart. His failure to bid two clubs over one heart suggests at most three clubs. So, his distribution is likely 3-1-6-3 or 3-1-7-2. Given this information, how can the contract be defeated?

To begin with, partner must have a diamond trick to have any chance of beating the contract. If so, what must declarer have in high cards to bid three diamonds? He has a singleton heart. He has six or seven diamonds missing at most one honor. He has three spades. So, he has either (1) the K-x-x of spades plus the ace and maybe also the queen of clubs or (2) the J-x-x of spades with the ace and queen of clubs.

In the first case, the contract is impregnable. If I play the spade nine, declarer simply knocks out partner's diamond trick and loses three spades and a diamond.

In the second case, the contract will also make if I play the nine of spades. Declarer wins the first spade with the jack and attacks diamonds, again losing only three spades and a diamond. However, if I win the first spade and return one, the contract can no longer be made. Partner will win with the king of spades and make a nice switch to a heart (which Mike did), cooking declarer's goose. If he ducks, I win with the queen of hearts, revert to spades and we take three spades, a heart and a diamond. On the other hand, if he wins with the ace of hearts, we take two spades, two hearts and a diamond.

Here is the complete deal:

Mike
- ♠ Kxxx
- ♡ xx
- ◊ Qxx
- ♣ xxxx

West
- ♠ Jxx
- ♡ x
- ◊ AKJ10xx
- ♣ AQx

```
      N
  W       E
      S
```

East
- ♠ Qx
- ♡ AJ109xx
- ◊ xx
- ♣ Kxx

me
- ♠ A109x
- ♡ KQ8x
- ◊ xx
- ♣ xxx

Adaptability

All bridge players are competitive. Most overrate their games and underrate those of others. Furthermore, most of those who overrate their games are bull-headed. They will argue that their convention or technique is best simply because a so-called expert touts it, and will therefore refuse to try yours. However, they will usually be unable to give adequate reasons (in fact, most will refuse to discuss it lest they reveal their own ignorance) and are ultimately handicapping themselves. Learning from others is the best, if not the only, way to improve. If you are not open to suggestions, even criticisms, then your game will stagnate. Adaptability is essential.

You don't have to agree with feedback, but you must listen non-defensively and then make your own analysis based on whatever new information you have received. A valid and commendable reason to play a convention is to gain experience with it so as to open-mindedly determine whether or not you want to use it, as well as to learn how to defend against it. On the other hand, don't cling to a convention merely because you "like its cute and catchy name", or because you've "always played it", or because "a terrific player said it was good" or because "everybody uses it". It would surprise you (but not me) how many of the so-called improved modern conventions don't hold up under close scrutiny.

S. J. Simon, in *Design for Bidding*, proposes the correct criteria for evaluating the worth of any convention. This is the same Simon who wrote the more famous *Why You Lose At Bridge*. To judge adequately the usefulness of a convention, you must consider:

- Its effect on other types of hands.

- Its comparative frequency of occurrence among rivals.

- Its obedience or otherwise to the Principle of the Lesser Risk (of reaching or beating Absolute Par).

- Whether or not it actually works on the hands on which it is used.

As Simon points out, anyone can construct a perfect hand (as well as a perfect anti-hand) for any convention. But bridge is a game of percentages, so don't dogmatically write a convention in indelible ink on your convention card just because it happens to land you a top board, not until you see how many bottom boards it also leads you to. Conversely, don't throw it out just because you get a bottom until after you see how many tops it brings.

In addition to being open to cogent arguments against your favorite bids, being adaptable also means that you are willing to experiment with various methods and settings and observe your results. Experts who are proficient at both duplicate and money rubber bridge, who compete against both strong and weak opponents, who play both IMPs and matchpoints and who are well versed in many systems (especially strong club and weak notrump systems) have a decided edge.

If you really want to improve your game, I recommend that you spend some time playing the fewest possible bidding and signaling conventions. Needless to say, rubber bridge provides an excellent venue in which to do this. You will be thrown into the water without a life jacket and will have to learn to fend for yourself. Being unable to use conventions as crutches you will be forced to draw more inferences from your partner's bids and play. You will also be better able to estimate the strengths and deficiencies of any of your customary conventions and can hone your system accordingly. Furthermore, you will be more prepared to play with a new partner whose system is different than yours. If you learn to visualize what partner is trying to tell you without needing a clear road map, you will be better able to draw subtle inferences, recognize nuances and make good competitive decisions when you do switch back to your favorite full-blown system.

You will be surprised how relaxing it is to not have to tax your memory with gazillions of conventions. As humans, we are all prone to an occasional lapse of memory. As has been pointed out by many, the cost of a bidding misunderstanding is usually enough to counterbalance any gains that your system brings you during a bridge session. Here is a humorously excruciating example:

At a Portland regional, Pat Dunn and I were playing together in a Swiss team for either the second or third time. As we were discussing our system, it became increasingly apparent to us that our bidding styles were quite different, so we agreed to play a patchwork system. Since Pat was a seasoned duplicate player with a vast knowledge of conventions and I was an old-time rubber bridge player who had not kept up with modern bidding, he kindly agreed to do most of the compromising. In all fairness, I must admit that this forced him to vary from his conventions of choice considerably more than it did me. As a result, he was in somewhat unfamiliar territory. At my suggestion, one of the conventions that we agreed to play was that, after a 1NT opener, a transfer to hearts followed by a bid of two spades showed 4-4-4-1 distribution with an as-yet-unspecified singleton.

Near the end of the match I picked up

♠ Axxx   ♡ x   ◇ AQxx   ♣ Qxxx

Pat opened 1NT and I bid two diamonds, intending to follow with two spades. Much to my dismay, LHO bid two spades over my two diamond bid and partner bid three hearts! We had not discussed what to do in the event of interference, so I was left to my own devices to figure out how to best extricate myself from this unexpected development.

It occurred to me that, if I bid three spades, partner might have spade strength and bid 3NT, which I would pass with a sigh of relief. Unfortunately his spade holding was much too weak to bid 3NT, so he returned to four hearts. I was still not overly perturbed since, if partner had weak spades, five of a minor could easily be better than 3NT. So, I bid 4NT, which was clearly RKC Blackwood, hoping that Pat's controls were such that he would respond in a minor suit. No such luck — he bid five spades! Being an optimist, I now hoped that, since I had a pretty good hand, he might be able to make six of a minor despite his wasted strength in hearts. Furthermore, even if he went down one, we might still push the board if 3NT also fails. With fingers crossed, I bid 5NT. Since we were playing specific kings, there was an excellent chance that Pat would bid six of a minor, which he did.

When I passed, Pat's befuddled look was enough to push me over the edge; I could restrain myself no longer and burst out laughing. At this point, it finally dawned on Pat what had happened. When the dummy came down, he rolled up his sleeves and proceeded to play the deal superbly to escape for down one. I wish I could report that this tale had a happy ending but, alas, we lost ten IMPs on the board. As it turned out, he had opened 1NT with a singleton spade! I don't advocate this in general and on this particular deal it greatly increased the odds of the opponents interfering, which led to our downfall.

Partner's signals should be treated as recommendations, not commands. If, based on the information at your disposal, you have a better idea as to the right defense than partner does, feel free to disregard his suggestion. Signals are a poor substitute for logic. Here are two examples:

Playing with Gard Hays in a recent regional Swiss team event, I encountered the following deal:

Neither vul.

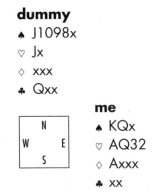

dummy
♠ J1098x
♡ Jx
◊ xxx
♣ Qxx

me
♠ KQx
♡ AQ32
◊ Axxx
♣ xx

West	North	East	South
2NT	pass	3♡[1]	pass
3♠	pass	3NT	all pass

1. Transfer.

Opening lead: ♡10

I won the opening heart lead with the ace and continued with the queen and the three, won by declarer with the king. Declarer next played diamonds. I took my ace on the third round, at which time partner carefully discarded the two of spades. What now?

Without hesitation I led the spade king! This elicited a barely perceptible look of disgust from partner. Declarer won with the ace and, after some thought, continued spades. I won the queen and calmly cashed the setting heart trick. Partner, upon discovering that I held the missing heart, gave me a nod of approval. Here is the complete deal:

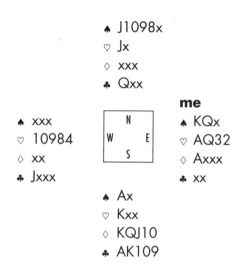

There are two reasons to play the king of spades. First, if you play your fourth heart, partner will win it and will have to lead a spade rather than a club to have any chance to beat the contract. Second, playing the spade king misleads declarer. It creates the impression that East started with only three hearts and, combined with partner's discard of the spade two, it confirms that East started with K-Q-x of spades. Declarer therefore (mistakenly) believes that he can safely play on spades.

Note that had I made a passive return of a diamond, declarer would have had no choice but to try to find his ninth trick in clubs. Moreover, given partner's shortness in diamonds, declarer may well have successfully finessed the jack.

Playing with Helen Abbott at a sectional in Seattle, I held the following hand:

Both vul.

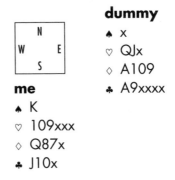

dummy
- ♠ x
- ♡ QJx
- ◊ A109
- ♣ A9xxxx

me
- ♠ K
- ♡ 109xxx
- ◊ Q87x
- ♣ J10x

West	North	East	South
1♠	pass	2♣	pass
2◊	pass	3♣	pass
3NT	all pass		

Opening lead: low heart

I played the nine of hearts on the opening lead. West won with the king and played a low diamond to the ace, on which Helen played the king. Another diamond was led from the dummy, taken by my queen, partner discarding the two of spades, whereupon I immediately led the spade king! Helen looked disappointed, but realized the efficacy of my play in the subsequent discussion at the bar over a beer.

Here is the complete deal:

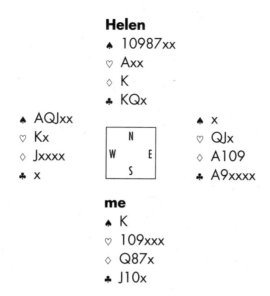

Helen
- ♠ 10987xx
- ♡ Axx
- ◇ K
- ♣ KQx

West
- ♠ AQJxx
- ♡ Kx
- ◇ Jxxxx
- ♣ x

```
      N
   W     E
      S
```

East
- ♠ x
- ♡ QJx
- ◇ A109
- ♣ A9xxxx

me
- ♠ K
- ♡ 109xxx
- ◇ Q87x
- ♣ J10x

Partner, correctly from her perspective, wanted me to shift to a club. As you can see, this enables West to easily make the contract. A heart return by me would succeed only if partner wins with the ace and switches to a spade (unlikely) instead of the king of clubs. The king of spades, however, dooms declarer by removing his entry to his hand before he has time to unblock the diamond suit.

Blindly following a 'standard' carding convention without also applying logic can often lead you astray. Let's look at a couple of situations:

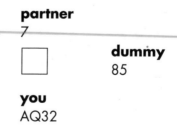

partner
7

dummy
85

you
AQ32

Suppose partner leads a seven against 3NT, dummy tables 8-5, and you hold A-Q-3-2. After winning with the ace, what do you return?

The right play is the queen, not the two, even though conventional wisdom says to return fourth best of partner's led suit. By the rule of eleven, declarer has only one card higher than the eight, so when you return the queen, your partner will be looking at the remaining high cards and will know the suit is running. On the other hand, if you return the two, partner should play you for a doubleton and may discontinue the suit. For instance, if he has led from K-J-9-7-4 and you return the two, then when the ten appears, partner will think that declarer started with Q-10-6-3 instead of doubleton 10-6. He will discontinue if he thinks the spade queen is declarer's ninth trick.

Playing in a recent regional pair event, I picked up the following hand:

Neither vul.

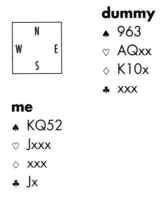

dummy
- ♠ 963
- ♡ AQxx
- ◇ K10x
- ♣ xxx

me
- ♠ KQ52
- ♡ Jxxx
- ◇ xxx
- ♣ Jx

West	North	East	South
1NT	pass	2♣	pass
2◇	pass	3NT	all pass

Opening lead: ♠J

What spade do you play at Trick 1? Partner would not lead the jack without the ten unless he was leading from a doubleton; however, you know from the bidding that he has at least three spades, since declarer has denied four. For the same reason, you know that declarer has at most three spades and partner knows you have at least four. So your right play is clearly the queen!

Why? Since partner is marked with at least J-10-x of spades, the queen is perfectly safe. Furthermore, since partner knows you have at least four, you must have the king or else the queen would make no sense. On the other hand, the five from you could be from various holdings. Here is the complete deal:

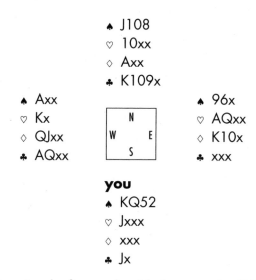

♠ J108
♡ 10xx
♢ Axx
♣ K109x

♠ Axx
♡ Kx
♢ QJxx
♣ AQxx

♠ 96x
♡ AQxx
♢ K10x
♣ xxx

you
♠ KQ52
♡ Jxxx
♢ xxx
♣ Jx

Suppose West wins the first spade with the ace, as he did on the actual deal. If you have played the ambiguous five, partner might think that declarer started with ♠A-K-Q and ♣Q-x-x. If he thinks so, he will make a disastrous shift to a low club when he gets in with the ace of diamonds.

The queen sends a clear message that you started with at least four spades headed by the K-Q, as long as partner draws the obvious inferences.

Judgment

Bidding judgment is the art of knowing when to save, when to double, when to bid one more if pushed, how high to preempt and making other similar decisions in competitive auctions. In other words, you must know how to properly evaluate both the offensive and defensive trick-taking potential of your hand. There is only one way to develop bidding judgment: play lots of deals with and against opponents who are better than you are and listen to their advice until you begin to get the hang of it. In this as well as in other areas, reading can take you only so far. You can't rely exclusively on so-called rules or maxims, especially the 'law' of total tricks. This is not a law at all; it is merely a poor substitute for good judgment. One useful general rule is that *the five-level belongs to the opponents*. However, even this rule has exceptions and you must be able to recognize them when they occur.

Don't be embarrassed to go for an occasional number. While the opponents are chortling, you can take solace in the knowledge that if you never go for a number, you aren't bidding enough. The secret is to keep the success ratio near 85%; no more, no less. If you manage this, you will be way ahead of the game and can afford a disaster or two. Practice will enable you to develop a sense for when to save. At the game level, be aggressive, but not foolhardy. Remember that if the cards are unfavorably placed for you, then they are favorably placed for the opponents. So, if you go down two or three tricks, they can probably make game, or maybe even slam. Aces can never be unfavorably placed, though, so don't save if you have aces. Hands with aces are defensive hands.

The first question to ask about any hand is whether or not it is more suitable for offense or defense. The answer to this question should determine your bidding strategy on every deal throughout every auction. Let's study this in detail.

Offensive hands

Offensive hands are distributional hands. I define a powerful offensive hand as one having a total of ten or more cards in two suits. In other words:

- any eight-card or longer suit
- 7-6-0-0, 7-5-1-0, 7-4-2-0, 7-4-1-1, 7-3-3-0, 7-3-2-1
- 6-6-1-0, 6-5-2-0, 6-5-1-1, 6-4-3-0, 6-4-2-1
- 5-5-3-0, 5-5-2-1

Unless your hand is defensive as well as offensive, adopt a preemptive approach with these hands in *competitive* or *potentially competitive* auctions at equal or favorable vulnerability. If you have a second suit of at least five cards (treat a strong four-card suit like a five-card suit when you are 6-4), in competitive auctions at equal or favorable vulnerability, and sometimes even at unfavorable vulnerability, bid according to the following rules:

(1) Bid *quickly* to the maximum level which you think you might make.

(2) If pushed, keep bidding beyond this level until you expect to set the opponents (see Rule 5).

(3) Show your second suit if you have not already done so whenever partner has not supported your first suit. (In non-competitive auctions, however, it is usually best to rebid a six-card or longer major before showing a four-card minor if you have a weak hand, especially at matchpoints.)

(4) If partner has supported your first suit, only bid your second suit to suggest a lead or to help your side decide whether or not any cards either of you might hold in the second suit are likely to cash on defense.

(5) After observing the first four rules, your side should stop bidding and double whenever either of you can reasonably expect to cash enough tricks to set the opponents.

There are exceptions, but if you start with these rules and hone them while you gain experience, you will come out on top more often than with any other starting approach, including the inferior 'law' of total tricks. Here are two typical competitive situations:

(i) At equal vulnerability you hold

♠ — ♡ AQ9xxx ◇ xx ♣ Q10xxx

RHO opens one diamond. Here you have *eleven* cards in two suits — what do you bid?

Bid four hearts, planning to bid five clubs if the opponents get to four undoubled spades. If you are doubled in four hearts, *don't* run to five clubs. Usually opponents are doubling with high cards, not a defensive trump stack, in which case you may make at the four-level but not at the five-level. On these kinds of hands, if you can't make four hearts, you are likely to be just as bad off or worse at a higher level in clubs, unless your partner has four or more. If he does, then the opponents have missed a fit of their own which they will discover if you run.

(ii) You are 5-5 and partner raises your first suit (a major) to two. What do you bid?

Jump to game with any hand in which you have no slam interest. With a strong offensive hand like this one, you will make more often than you might expect. Even if you can't, the opponents can probably make a four-level contract, so you should try to shut them out of the auction. If the opponents bid after your jump to four, take the push to five, unless you are reasonably sure you can beat them. For deceptive reasons, don't bother bidding your second suit unless the conditions of rule (4) apply.

When the auction is unlikely to be competitive, different rules apply. Suppose you hold six spades and four clubs and open one spade. In a *game-forcing* sequence, it is better to bid your four-card suit at your second turn rather than rebidding your six-card suit. For instance, if partner responds to your one spade opener with a game-forcing two diamond bid, then bid three clubs, not two spades, and plan to rebid your spades next. On the other hand, if partner responds with 1NT, bid two spades with a minimum.

Defensive hands

Defensive hands are those that contain lots of quick tricks (aces and kings). Obviously you don't want to preempt or save with these hands since you are on the lookout for an opportunity to make a penalty double. By going slowly with defensive hands, you make it easier for the opponents to compete when they shouldn't. You can afford to take your time to explore for your best spot. Don't be overly ambitious; when faced with a marginal decision, it is usually better to underbid than overbid with any defensive hand, even if it happens to be an offensive hand as well. Let's take a look at a few practical examples:

(i) You should avoid making superaccepts after Jacoby transfer bids. You are more likely to end up too high than too low, with a frequency that doesn't justify trying for the game bonus (especially if not vulnerable).

(ii) Similarly, with a balanced hand having less than a good 12 points, don't raise partner's 1NT rebid to 2NT — again, you are more likely to finish too high than too low. With balanced hands, it usually takes a full opener opposite a full opener to make game. Along the same lines, if partner is a passed hand, opener should not seek game with less than a very good 14 points.[1]

(iii) Don't make a *marginal* jump shift or jump rebid as opener; it is better to take a conservative approach. If partner's hand is only worth one bid, it is much more likely that you will get too high than that you will miss game.

---

1. Remember this when reading my version of reverse Drury in the section on conventions.

Evaluate your defensive trick-taking potential when considering whether or not to open with a balanced hand. It is a good idea always to have at least two quick tricks. If partner can count on this, he will be better able to decide when to double the opponents in competitive auctions. So, use this as a guide when deciding whether or not to open marginal hands. For example, you should always open

♠ Axx ♡ xxx ◇ AKxx ♣ xxx

whereas

♠ QJx ♡ Qxx ◇ AJxx ♣ Qxx

is a pass.

You should also evaluate your defensive trick-taking potential when considering whether or not to respond to partner's one-level opener. *Always* respond with an ace, but be reluctant to bid with a balanced 6 points consisting of queens and jacks unless you have support for partner's suit.

CHAPTER 2

Tips

One of the best books I have ever read and one I strongly recommend is *Design For Bidding* by S. J. Simon, written in 1949. Although bidding theory has changed dramatically over the last half century with the introduction of numerous artificial bids, it does not necessarily follow that bidding methods are any better today than they were thirty years ago. In my opinion, for the most part they have gotten worse! As Simon explains, scientific conventions cannot keep pace with the number of possibilities, and the lack of deception engendered by attempts at precise bidding usually helps the defense more often than science helps the offense. That the early theory of natural bidding is frequently superior is evidenced by its durability. Simon's ideas have been around for a long time, but they have stood the test of time. These methods have been developed from logic and experience rather than inspiration.

Par Value

More specifically, on the subject of preempts, Simon explains the extremely valuable concept of par value — the result which represents the optimum *simultaneous* result for the two sides. By attempting to reach your maximum result, you often jeopardize your chances of achieving at least absolute par value, the true yardstick by which to measure the result on any given deal.

Here's an example (both sides non-vulnerable). If you can make twelve tricks in spades and the opponents can make eleven tricks in hearts, your maximum value is +980 and theirs is +450. But the *absolute par value* on the deal is +300 for you and -300 for the opponents. Opening four spades rates to be the best chance to beat par value. If you manage to buy the deal at four spades, you are better off in the long run than getting to slam scientifically and inducing your opponents to save.

Simon's book has many illuminating examples of preempts and the superiority of 'non-scientific' bidding. You may not agree with him, but your game will improve if you at least study his point of view.

Doubles

Failing to make, or unwisely pulling, a penalty double has lost more money and IMPs than anything else. The same is also true of matchpoints, especially since it has become fashionable for opponents to make marginal overcalls at the one-level knowing that they are unlikely to be penalized whenever the opponents play negative doubles. Negative doubles are essential in any five-card major system in order to find 4-4 fits, but enough is lost to make me prefer four-card majors at money rubber bridge. There is a significant difference between a penalty double and a penalty pass. Too often, especially (but not exclusively) if your partner is not an expert, he will fail to reopen with a double when you most want him to, whereas he would gladly sit if your immediate double were for penalty rather than for takeout. When playing negative rather than positive doubles, the most frequent situations in which you will lose the opportunity to seriously penalize the opponents occur when opener holds either a two-suited hand (with which he will usually reopen by bidding his second suit) or a minimum hand with three cards in the opponents' suit (with which he will usually pass).

If your opponents never make a doubled contract, then you are not doubling enough. As was the case with saves, the secret is to keep the success ratio near 85%. I suggest that most of your doubles be penalty oriented. One exception is maximal (game-try) doubles (recommended) since they are essentially card-showing and your partner will often pass for penalty. In most cases, however, use a minimum of artificial doubles, and then only if you feel they are necessary. Artificial doubles that are particularly ill advised are support doubles (notwithstanding that their purported inventor, Eric Rodwell, is a top expert), support redoubles, takeout doubles of natural bids by an opponent after your partner has opened 1NT and high-level negative doubles.

On the subject of penalty doubles, even though I advocate using them freely, I strongly recommend the following rule: be very reluctant to make or sit for a penalty double if you have *unmentioned* trump support for partner, especially if the opponents are below game. As a corollary to this rule, make every effort to support partner at your first reasonable opportunity.

Example. As South, you pick up

♠ xxxx ♡ xx ◇ Kxxx ♣ xxx

The auction proceeds as follows:

N-S vul.

West	North	East	South
		1♣	pass
1♡	1♠	2♡	?

Bid two spades! Your partner has a good hand if he bids freely when vulnerable between two bidding opponents. If you don't raise and partner subsequently doubles when West bids four hearts, you are faced with an unsolvable dilemma. You will have no idea whether to bid four spades or pass and hope four hearts is going down. On the other hand, you can get off the hook by raising spades immediately. Partner knows you can't have much when he has a good hand and both opponents are bidding, so he won't hang you. Now, having alerted partner that his spade winners may not cash, you can comfortably leave in his double.

Once you have made that raise of partner's suit, you can relax knowing that much of your job has been done. In competitive auctions in which you have already supported partner's suit, don't take a *marginal* action if your partner has another bid coming; instead, wait to see what he does. You should only preempt your partner's decision if your action is clear. In particular, *never* pull partner's penalty doubles at the five-level unless you are right (according to the result)! One extremely important example of a clear action that is frequently not taken is a double from weakness, which alerts partner to pull at his own risk. Consider this deal, where you hold:

♠ xx ♡ Qxxx ◇ Qxx ♣ AJxx

Both vul.

West	North	East	South
	1♡	2♠	3♡
4♠	5♡	5♠	?

Double is a clear action! If you pass, you invite your partner to bid six hearts, which you certainly don't want to do with this hand.
So in summary:

- Prefer to play most doubles as penalty.

- Raise partner whenever you can reasonably do so.

- Having done so, leave competitive decisions to partner unless your action is clear-cut.

Notrump Openers

When deciding whether or not to open 1NT as opposed to one of a suit, experts generally focus on suit texture, quick versus slow tricks, spot cards, stoppers in all suits and other relatively unimportant considerations, such as holding at least three cards in the other major whenever you open 1NT with a five-card major. This is misguided. I recommend the following rule: if you can find some justification, *no matter how slight*, to open 1NT — do it! The reason is *ease of bidding*, a far more important criterion than any of the above.

Most of us have a potent arsenal of weapons that *only come into play after a 1NT opener*, i.e. some version of Stayman, transfers, Smolen, precise ranges for invitational sequences, bids to show or ask about minors, bids to show two-suited hands, bids to show 4-4-4-1 distribution, Lebensohl in competition, etc, etc. If you have game or slam, it is much easier to reach the right contract if partner immediately knows your strength and distribution within a well-defined range and can bring your notrump conventions into play. He can then take charge of the auction and, after a few exploratory bids, will be in a good position to determine the final contract.

At some point in any game-going or slam-going auction someone has to take charge. Obviously, the logical candidate is the one who has the most information about partner's hand, since he has less additional information to gather. The earlier he can take charge, the more time he will have to pinpoint partner's cards and distribution. After a 1NT opener, partner becomes the one in control and can start exploring as early as the two-level (the ideal situation)! Even with no game or slam in sight, you will more likely reach the right partscore after starting with 1NT.

Example. At matchpoints in a 2/1 system, you hold

♠ Kxxxx ♡ AQ ◇ Ax ♣ Kxxx

By the experts' criteria, this hand cries out for an opening bid of one spade. But if you open one spade, it is no longer possible to play

1NT. Furthermore, what do you bid if partner responds 1NT (forcing) and over your two clubs he bids two diamonds? Most likely you pass and there you are, playing in a two-level minor-suit contract rather than the 1NT you wish you were in (especially at matchpoints).

Furthermore, the deal is probably being played from the wrong side. More information has been relayed to the opponents for finding the killing opening lead than had the auction gone 1NT, all pass.

I like to define a 1NT opener as any hand with no singleton, no six-card suit, no less than 15 points (or 14 with a five-card suit) and no more than 17 points with no five-card suit (with 17 and a five-card suit, open one of your suit and plan to rebid 2NT). Avoiding a 1NT opener with a six-card suit is especially important. If your strength is concentrated in your six-card suit, you will lack the defensive strength partner will play you for when making a penalty double. If your six-card suit is headed by the jack, however, opening 1NT is acceptable. Within these limits, almost anything goes. If you have an unstopped suit, don't be deterred; if partner passes 1NT, you will have plenty of losers to pitch while the opponents are taking the first five tricks. Likewise, don't worry if you are 5-4-2-2 or have no spot higher than a six. The one exception to this is a 5-4-2-2 hand when most of your strength is concentrated in your two longest suits. With these hands you can pretend to 'add a card' to your strongest suit. Then the hand becomes an offensive hand (since you now have ten cards in two suits) as well as a defensive one and should be opened in a suit.

Even more strongly, I advocate opening 2NT (or two clubs followed by 2NT) with a five-card major if your point count is right (again, add one point for a five-card suit), in conjunction with puppet Stayman. Perhaps the experts know when to open one of a major rather than 2NT with these hands, but I confess I don't. I'd rather have my cake and eat it too. This approach allows me to do so while retaining the previously mentioned advantage, ease of bidding. One potent convention available over 2NT openers (or two clubs followed by 2NT) is a slightly modified version of four-way transfers, provided you are willing always to go through puppet Stayman on the way to 3NT. I cover this in detail in the section on conventions.

Patience is a Virtue

These days it has become fashionable to compete at every opportunity. As a result "fools rush in where angels fear to tread". The best approach whenever you know you will have another chance to bid is often to wait until you have gained more information, unless you have a weak offensive hand, as defined earlier, or the boss suit. Of course, you should never wait to show trump support for partner. We have already seen some examples of this, notably the first two example hands in the section on deception and the second one in the section on doubles. Let's explore some other common situations where this tip is relevant.

It is extremely dangerous to bounce into an auction between two bidding opponents, each of whose hands is as yet unlimited. By waiting to see how the subsequent auction develops before jumping in, you gain a large measure of safety. Suppose you hold this hand:

♠ Q109xx ♡ Kx ◇ Qxx ♣ KQx

Both vul.

West	North	East	South
1♣	pass	1♡	?

Most players today would bid one spade. The lead-directing value of this bid is dubious at best, but a penalty double by opener would be a disaster! (As an example, give opener the hand shown in the section on support doubles.) If partner holds as few as 3 HCP, the opponents will probably not have game whenever opener holds four spades. Even if they do, they probably won't bid it. With your hand, however, you will be lucky if you go for only 500. If you make the correct call of 'pass' instead, then only good things will happen.

Suppose the auction proceeds as follows:

Both vul.

West	North	East	South
1♣	pass	1♡	*pass*
2♡ or 1NT	pass	pass	?

Now you can bid two spades, knowing partner has some cards and probably at least two spades.

Alternatively, suppose LHO bids one spade over his partner's one heart.

West	North	East	South
1♣	pass	1♡	*pass*
1♠	pass	pass	?

Now you will breathe a sigh of relief that you stayed out of the bidding.

Suppose LHO bids 2NT over his partner's one heart.

West	North	East	South
1♣	pass	1♡	*pass*
2NT	pass	pass	?

Now, not only will you be happy that you stayed out of the bidding, you will also welcome a club lead from partner if that is his choice, rather than a spade lead.

On the other hand, you *should* bid one spade with this hand if you are not between two bidding opponents, namely whenever RHO opens the bidding. There are three major differences that tip the scales in favor of the immediate overcall. First, the opening hand is in front of you instead of behind you. Second, LHO cannot make a penalty double if the opponents play negative doubles. Opener will frequently not reopen with a double, and even if he does, partner has a choice of two suits to pull to if he so desires rather than one if you are between two bidding opponents. Third, whereas you know you will get another chance to bid if you are between two bidding opponents, in this situation, opener's partner may pass and your partner probably won't reopen with less than nine points even if he has a spade fit.

Another common situation in which waiting is right is when you hold a weak hand with a six-card or longer suit and you know you will have another chance to bid. There are several variations on this theme. One is when partner opens the bidding and your RHO overcalls. Suppose you hold the following:

♠ x ♡ QJ10xxxx ◇ xx ♣ xxx

Both vul.

West	North	East	South
	1♠	2◇	?

If you play negative doubles, then you should pass rather than preempting immediately in hearts. Partner will reopen with a double most of the time, after which you can bid two or three hearts depending on the vulnerability. If partner reopens with two spades instead, you can pass and stay out of trouble, unless two spades gets doubled. In that case, you can run to three hearts and be no worse off than if you had bid hearts immediately. Here is another variation:

♠ Q10xxxxx ♡ xx ◇ xx ♣ xx

Both vul.

West	North	East	South
1◇	1♡	2♣	?

Again, pass is best. Now when you bid spades at your next turn, partner will play you for a weak hand with long spades.

What is a Good Suit?

Nearly all bridge books will at some point say that in some situations you need a good suit in order to bid it. This book is no exception, but unlike most books, it will define precisely what is meant by the term *good suit*. Is A-Q-x-x a good four-card suit? Is A-Q-10-x-x a good five-card suit? Is Q-J-9-8-x-x a good six-card suit? Is A-x-x-x-x-x-x a good seven-card suit? Are all eight-card suits good? What about nine-card suits?

It would seem, incorrectly, that no general definition of a good suit can exist which covers suits of all lengths. Without such a definition, however, any treatment must either provide separate definitions for suits of different length — which would be quite tedious and has therefore never been attempted (to my knowledge) — or else lack clarity. So, I offer the following perfectly good general definition that will apply throughout the remainder of the book. *Pretend that your suit is trumps, that your partner is void and that the suit splits as well as possible. If it is at most a two-loser suit, then it is a good suit for its length.*

Let's see how this rule works in practice. We will ignore suits with fewer than three cards, since nobody really cares if they are good or not.

(1) Three-card suits. Using my rule, it is easy to list all good three-card suits. They are any suit headed by the ace, the K-Q, the K-J-10 or the Q-J-10. Any other suit is a three-loser suit.

(2) Four-card suits. We can also easily list all good four-card suits. They are A-K-x-x, A-Q-J-x, A-Q-10-9, A-J-10-9, K-Q-J-x, K-Q-10-9, K-J-10-9 and Q-J-10-9.

(3) Five-card suits. If we apply our assumption that these split 4-4, the good five-card suits are the same as the good four-card suits but with an extra card (the extra card can't be a loser if the suit splits 4-4). They are A-K-x-x-x, A-Q-J-x-x, A-Q-10-9-x, A-J-10-9-x, K-Q-J-x-x, K-Q-10-9-x, K-J-10-9-x and Q-J-10-9-x.

(4) Six-card suits. Following the same reasoning, if we assume that these split 4-3, then the good ones are the good five-card suits with an extra card. They are A-K-x-x-x-x, A-Q-J-x-x-x, A-Q-10-9-x-x, A-J-10-9-x-x, K-Q-J-x-x-x, K-Q-10-9-x-x, K-J-10-9-x-x and Q-J-10-9-x-x.

(5) Seven-card suits. Here we assume a 3-3 split, so the good ones are A-x-x-x-x-x-x, K-Q-x-x-x-x-x, K-J-10-x-x-x-x and Q-J-10-x-x-x-x.

(6) Eight-card suits. Assuming a 3-2 split, the good ones the same as the seven-card suits with an extra card. They are A-x-x-x-x-x-x-x, K-Q-x-x-x-x-x-x, K-J-10-x-x-x-x-x and Q-J-10-x-x-x-x-x. If you are optimistic, you can also include K-J-9-8-x-x-x-x and Q-J-9-8-x-x-x-x, since you have a 40% chance of finding a doubleton ten, which would limit you to two losers.

(7) Nine-card or longer suits. All nine-card or longer suits are good under our assumed conditions. No defender can hold more than two and therefore can't possibly take more than two tricks.

Since we have exhibited all of the good suits, why not merely memorize the list and dispense with the definition? First, the definition explains how the list is arrived at. Second, and more importantly, it is much easier to remember and apply one definition than to memorize 38 different suits!

Our focus up to now has been to distinguish good suits from 'bad' ones. Needless to say, the longer a good suit is, the more tricks it will produce. There are also varying degrees of good suits. The fewer losers there are, under our assumptions, the better the suit. There are no-loser suits, one-loser suits, two-loser suits, three-loser suits and suits between these. The optional eight-card suits given above (under 6) are examples of in-between suits — they are 2.6 loser suits. The differences all revolve around suit texture (the presence of intermediate cards such as nines and eights), an important guide that has been subsumed under our definition of good suits. Suit texture can also be useful in helping to differentiate between good suits and very good suits.

Directing the Lead

I mentioned earlier in a brief discussion on overcalling, that sometimes the rationale for getting into the auction is to tell partner what to lead. Let's explore that a little further.

One-level Overcalls

When considering an immediate one-level overcall with a relatively weak hand, you must weigh the necessity of suggesting to partner that you can tolerate only the lead of your suit against the risk of suffering a hefty penalty. Naturally, the likelihood that your partner, rather than you, will end up on opening lead is a major consideration. Since ineffective opening leads have caused more marginal contracts to be made than anything else, the risk of going for a number is usually worth taking, especially against a five-card major system where the previously discussed deficiencies of negative doubles are in play. Even so, be more cautious against strong opponents and/or with unfavorable vulnerability. In any case, if you hold eight or more points and a suit with four honor cards, always overcall at the one-level, even with a four-card suit! If you hold 9 to 11 points and your suit is Q-10-x-x-x or worse, don't bother to overcall (wait and see if it is safe to balance later). Hands between these two ranges require judgment but, if it's close, give the higher weight to opening-lead considerations, i.e. not only the strength of your suit, but also the unsuitability of your hand for any other lead. Needless to say, with this approach, partner will need a compelling reason not to lead your suit!

Two-level Overcalls

Two-level jump overcalls serve a preemptive purpose as well as lead-direction. They follow roughly the same criteria as a one-level overcall, except that you need at least six cards in your suit to make them.

However, for two-level *non-jump* overcalls, you also need significantly more strength, since the chance of being severely penalized is much higher. The opponents have an easier decision to make and your LHO's strength is as yet unknown. Furthermore, you are encouraging partner to compete, so even if *you* escape, partner may get penalized at a higher level. To make a two-level non-jump overcall, you need one of the following three types of hands:

- A near opening bid (or better) with a good six-card suit. Always make either a simple or jump overcall with a good six-card or longer major unless you are too strong (in which case it might be better to double first, especially with spades).

- At least 16 points if you only have a (good) five-card suit and your hand is not suitable for a takeout double

- A good opener with a five-card suit if you have two places to play and have a convention that allows you to play in either, although with these hands it is often better to wait and see what LHO does. Whenever LHO doesn't either raise his partner, pass, or bid 1NT, he will either bid one of your suits, in which case you now know to stay out of the auction, or he will bid the fourth suit, in which case you can make a takeout double on your next turn.

With other types of hands, don't overcall. Instead, wait until LHO reveals his strength and then balance if appropriate (as discussed in Patience is a Virtue).

Doubling for the lead

Lead-directing doubles are powerful weapons. Although the opportunities to use them occur infrequently, they lead to large swings when they do arise. You and your partner should have an agreement as to the meaning of every unusual or unexpected double. Everyone is familiar with the highly effective Lightner double, which asks partner to make an unusual lead (often dummy's first-bid suit) against a slam. The strength of this convention is that it prevents partner from making his natural lead whenever there is a better one. I propose that, for best results, *all* lead-directing doubles be based on this same principle – that the lead not be the suit that would have been normal without the double.

Let's consider some typical situations:

West	North	East	South
		1♠	2♡
3♣	pass	3NT	pass
pass	dbl	all pass	

You are South. What should you lead? Opinions vary as to what is best. But, consistent with the above principle, I recommend a club lead for the following reasons. Partner expects you to lead your suit rather than make a blind stab at something else. If he is happy with that, pass will suffice most of the time. So, double should suggest something else. On the given auction, a double by North would be too risky if dummy's clubs are running, so his double should imply control of the club suit and, accordingly, ask you to lead it.

West	North	East	South
		1♠	pass
4◊[1]	dbl	4♠	all pass

1. Splinter.

As South, what should you lead? Steve Sidell familiarized me with an agreement that I highly recommend — a double of a splinter asks for the lead of the lower-ranking unbid suit. On the given auction, doubling to suggest a diamond lead makes little sense since West is announcing diamond shortness. Furthermore, you should expect partner to lead a diamond on most deals. So, in conformance with our principle, a double should suggest something else.

West	North	East	South
		1NT	pass
3NT	dbl	all pass	

As South, what should you lead? Clearly this depends on your agreement with partner. The key point is that you should have an agreement! A double of any notrump contract at the two-level or higher when neither you nor the opponents have bid a suit should ask for the lead of a specific suit. This is sometimes known as an Elwell double and should be written on your convention card if you play it. I play that it asks for a heart lead, since the chance to use it will come up more often if it requests a specific *major*-suit lead. (The convention is more likely to apply when the opponents are short in one of the majors and have no need to bid Stayman, or a suit, which would nullify the convention.)

Here is a hand that I dream about one day playing in the finals of the Vanderbilt, while sitting East:

Both vul.

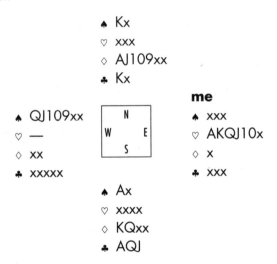

♠ Kx
♡ xxx
◇ AJ109xx
♣ Kx

me

♠ QJ109xx   ♠ xxx
♡ —   ♡ AKQJ10x
◇ xx   ◇ x
♣ xxxxx   ♣ xxx

♠ Ax
♡ xxxx
◇ KQxx
♣ AQJ

Our table

West	North	East	South
			1NT
pass	3NT	dbl*	pass
pass	4◇	pass	5◇
all pass			

Other table

West	North	East	South
			1NT
pass	3NT	all pass	

The result at our table: five diamonds down one.
The result at the other table: 3NT making five.
Net: +760 and 13 IMPs for us.

The Art of Cuebidding

By definition, a cuebid is the bid of any suit (other than trumps) by either player in a game-forcing auction after it is clear what trumps will be. Examples:

West	North	East	South
	1NT	pass	2♡
pass	2♠	pass	3♣

Three clubs is not a cuebid; it is a suit. The trump suit has not yet been set.

West	North	East	South
			1♠
pass	2◊[1]	pass	2♡
pass	2♠	pass	3♣

1. GF.

Three clubs is a cuebid. The trump suit has been set.

    Cuebidding has become a largely forgotten art. Most players abuse Blackwood by using it before they have sufficient information to place the contract, as is usually the case when they know only about controls. It seems as if the urge to jump to 4NT is ingrained in every bridge player at birth and has to be carefully rooted out. Unless partner has made a bid with a fairly well-defined distribution and point range (such as a weak two-bid or 1NT), don't *jump* to Blackwood or Gerber. Do so only when you are certain you will be able determine where the contract belongs knowing only how many controls partner has and, if he has a sufficient number, how many outside kings (or which specific kings) he holds. The primary danger you face with a hand big enough to warrant slam consideration is not that you will bid six and go down missing two controls (since

Blackwood alone will usually prevent this); the danger is that you will bid only six when you are cold for seven, or bid seven when you can make only six, or bid five when you can make only four (Blackwood alone will not usually prevent these).

There is no hurry to use Blackwood; it is always available once you reach the four-level, so why not use the lower levels to make some exploratory bids, notably cuebids? At the very least, doing so may keep you out of trouble whenever partner holds a useless void. Incidentally, the unnecessary bypassing of lower levels is also the reason why the modern principle of fast arrival (PFA) is inferior to the 'outdated' method of going slow.

Now let's look at the basics of effective cuebidding. You will have fewer potential problems if you play ace and king cuebids, but this discussion also applies if you don't. An initial cuebid by either player guarantees extra values. If your partner indicates game or slam interest by making a cuebid, your first responsibility is to tell him whether or not you are also interested. If you have a minimum for your bids up to this point do not cuebid (even if you have a control to show); instead, merely return to the agreed-upon suit at the cheapest level. If partner then makes another cuebid, you can fully cooperate, having already warned him that you have no extras. With this approach, cuebidding becomes more than merely a method of showing controls; it also serves the important purpose of showing whether or not you are at the top of the range for the bids you have already made. It goes without saying that any initial cuebid made during a game-forcing sequence invites slam and any cuebid made at the six-level invites seven.

There is no practical limit (other than bidding space) to the number of cuebids that can be made while probing for game or slam. Study the following prototypical auction:

West	North	East	South
			1♠
pass	2♣¹	pass	2◊
pass	2♠	pass	?

1. Game forcing.

If you now bid anything but 2NT or three spades, you show extras. (A new suit would be a cuebid with slam interest and four spades would show solid spades.) In any event, regardless of whether you show extras or not, if partner's next bid is either spades or notrump at the cheapest available level *he* shows a minimum. Any other bid by him shows extras and a hand strong enough to explore for slam even if you have shown a minimum. Subsequent cuebidding continues the search for slam and either partner is free to cooperate fully, even with a minimum, provided it has already been shown. At some point (usually at the four-level), it will become clear to one partner or the other whether or not to sign off, continue cuebidding, bid 4NT, or go directly to slam.

Unless you have a well-honed partnership, I suggest that cuebidding begin only if and when it is absolutely clear to both partners what the trump suit is going to be. Otherwise, the risk of landing in the wrong spot is too great. Incidentally, this same advice applies to RKC Blackwood. Playing with Steve Sidell in the Seattle regional I picked up:

♠ AKx ♡ AKxx ◇ A10xxx ♣ x

The auction proceeded as follows:

West	North	East	South
	Steve		Me
			1◇
pass	1♠	pass	2♡
pass	3◇	pass	3♠
pass	4◇	pass	4♡
pass	4NT	pass	?

Playing RKC Blackwood, what do you respond?

Some play that the trump suit is always the last suit bid, but we hadn't agreed to this. Furthermore, if partner were interested in playing spades, his diamonds might not be sufficient to cover my shabby suit. I finally decided that going down in a grand slam would be a near-bottom, whereas bidding six and making seven rated to be near average against a fair-to-mediocre field. So I bid six diamonds, which Steve corrected to six spades, holding

♠ QJ10xx ♡ x ◇ KQxx ♣ Axx

As you can see we had thirteen tricks off the top but, fortunately, my assessment was accurate. We got an above-average board by beating all the pairs who played six diamonds or failed to reach slam and tying all pairs who also played in six spades. Since then, Steve and I have had lengthy discussions about how we each might have bid our hands better and have, we hope, resolved the problem.

Opening Leads

As pointed out in the section on lead direction, the wrong opening lead has allowed more marginal contracts to be made than any other factor. It was also noted previously that you need a compelling reason not to lead your partner's suit when he has overcalled. When left to your own devices, there are many sound well-known principles at your disposal. I will discuss only a few of them.

Trump leads

Lew Mathe, a Los Angeles superstar in the 1950s and 60s, used to say with tongue in cheek, "Never lead trumps." Although this advice is obviously unwise, I recommend a slightly altered version: "Rarely lead a singleton or doubleton trump." There are only two situations in which it is best to ignore this rule. One is when a passive lead is called for and leading any other suit would be risky. Another is when the opponents have a known 5-5 trump fit and you have shortness or a stack in declarer's second suit. Although there may be a few other types of hands in which leading a doubleton trump will work out, the odds are against it.

Many players automatically lead trumps whenever they are long in declarer's side suit, but this is misguided. If you are short in trumps and opponents are in an eight- or nine-card fit, more often than not, you will cost partner a trump trick while at the same time preventing him from being able to overruff the dummy. Conversely, whenever it won't cost you a trick, you should almost always lead a trump with three if the opponents have bid and raised the suit, especially when they have opted to play in a suit after flirting with a notrump contract. Also lead a trump with four when in the same situation, unless you have a side suit that affords you a good opportunity to tap out the declarer.

Leads against suit contracts

Prevailing wisdom dictates the following: lead aggressively, especially against slams; go for taps with trump length and a side suit; it is safer to lead from a short king than from a long one (lead small from K-x through dummy's long suit to create the illusion that you have a singleton), etc. You are probably familiar with most of these. They all have merit; some more so than others. I don't have much to add except to emphasize that the advice always to lead aggressively is sound. Instead, with regard to opening leads against suits, I want to stress the importance of a much-neglected attribute — imagination. No other area of the game rewards a sterling application of imagination more handsomely than opening leads. No other area of the game affords a greater opportunity to exercise it. You can even use it profitably on the opening lead when you are declarer!

Here is an example provided by a well-known star of the 1950s. I am withholding his name because his ploy would be considered unethical under today's high standards.

```
        ♠ AQxx
        ♡ Ax
        ◇ AK
        ♣ KJ10xx
```

```
        ♠ KJ10xxx
        ♡ QJ
        ◇ xx
        ♣ Qxx
```

West	North	East	South
			2♠
pass	4NT	pass	5♣
pass	6♠	all pass	

Opening lead: ♡9

It was the last deal of the session and our opponents were two elderly ladies. They spent their time complaining about their poor game and seemed in a hurry to get this one over with. The star was having a good game and knew he would win the event with a near top board. He thought he was doomed when the nine of hearts was led, but his imagination soon sprang to the rescue. He proceeded to wait for what seemed to his unconcerned and impatient opponents like an eternity. When East's eyes started to glaze over, he snapped the queen of hearts onto the table in front of him!

This was immediately covered by East's king and won with dummy's ace. At this point, he hastily claimed twelve tricks, conceding only the ace of clubs, and put his hand back into the board. The ladies were so gratified that the session was finally over that they couldn't wait to sign the score and escape to the bar, paying so little attention to the deal that they never realized what the sequence of play to Trick 1 had actually been.

The most imaginative lead I have ever been privy to (unfortunately it was made against me with devastating effect) was against a four-heart contract. LHO led the two of spades, the suit his partner had bid. Dummy tabled K-x-x of spades and I, holding J-x-x, ducked. Imagine my surprise when RHO won with the queen, returned a spade to LHO's ace, got in with the ace of trumps and gave his partner a spade ruff for the setting trick! Needless to say, I was the only one in the room going down, justifying to anyone who would listen how I had failed to win a spade trick with the king when the ace was in front of it.

A final piece of advice: against any suit contract, whenever partner has bid a suit and you have raised with three (or more) headed by the king lead the king! This will rarely cost. On the other hand, in most cases when your partner holds the ace he can either overtake or let you win the first trick. The successful defense to many a deal hinges on who is on lead at Trick 2.

Leads against notrump

Against notrump slams, it is no secret that you should lead passively. Against games or partscores, the time-tested adage to lead fourth best from longest and strongest unless opponents have bid the suit is still excellent advice. It should not, however, be followed automatically. When you have no entries to your suit or your four-card suit is weak, consider eschewing the fourth best from longest and strongest rule. In these cases it is often best to try to find partner's suit or to attack one of dummy's bid or implied suits. A frequent occurrence is when dummy has bid Stayman and his partner has denied a major. If you hold a doubleton in a major suit, then partner will usually have at least four, so leading the suit is attractive, especially if you hold an honor (in which case I suggest you lead it).

Also, don't forget to draw inferences from what partner *doesn't* do. All else being equal don't try to find partner with a suit that he has failed to double when it has been bid artificially in front of him, i.e. don't expect partner to have good clubs if he has failed to double Stayman.

I am reminded of my favorite deal. In the 1960s I was playing with my brother Steve (an excellent technician) in a side game at Bridge Week. He was in 3NT holding ◊J-6 opposite ◊9-7 in the dummy. The opening leader was Abigail, a sweet lady who was midway through a series of beginning bridge lessons. Remembering one of her earlier lessons, she proudly led the two of diamonds, fourth best from her strongest suit. Partner, who had no diamond stopper, knew he was doomed. He played one of dummy's low cards and resignedly started to play the six from his hand on the first trick. Just as it touched the table, he realized that RHO had played the eight, which he could actually beat! He quickly pulled the six back, but it was too late. Abigail, who always played by the rules, stuck to her guns. She had learned her rights and indignantly refused to let Steve take back his play. Nevertheless, although Abigail's partner returned a diamond, there was still nothing the opponents could do to prevent us from getting a top board. Can you figure out why?

Here is the complete deal:

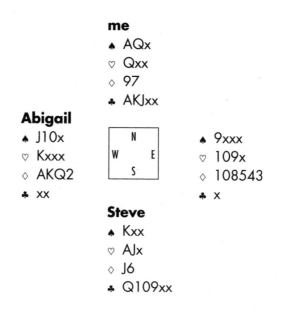

me
- ♠ AQx
- ♡ Qxx
- ◇ 97
- ♣ AKJxx

Abigail
- ♠ J10x
- ♡ Kxxx
- ◇ AKQ2
- ♣ xx

East
- ♠ 9xxx
- ♡ 109x
- ◇ 108543
- ♣ x

Steve
- ♠ Kxx
- ♡ AJx
- ◇ J6
- ♣ Q109xx

West	North	East	South
	1♣	pass	2NT
pass	3NT	all pass	

Opening lead: ◇2

Unfortunately for Abigail, she had not yet received the lesson on unblocking! Fourth best from this diamond holding did not turn out so well for her! This deal serves as a humorous reminder that bridge is too rich a game to be effectively contained within a set of axioms and conventions. In bridge, as well as in life, rules are made to be broken. Logic always trumps (forgive the pun) rigid adherence to traditional principles.

Defensive Signals

It is hard to imagine how the old-timers could have defeated many contracts before the advent of defensive signaling. Having said this, it is also hard to underestimate the value of the information that declarer gains from a defensive signal. For this reason, never give partner an unnecessary signal. If your partner is an expert he needs your help far less frequently than you might think; logic usually suffices. More 4-3 suits have been brought home via an anti-percentage finesse for a jack (as opposed to playing for a 3-3 split) due to a 'routine' defensive count signal than from any other cause. One of the hardest habits to break when making the transition to expert status is the urge to give partner the count at every opportunity.

It is usually impossible to convey an exact message with a single card; the best one can do is come as close as possible to this ideal. The best signaling conventions are those that convey the most information in the fewest number of cards, preferably one. The following recommendations all satisfy this principle and, so far as I can tell, do it in the most effective way.

Against notrump

Smith echo is a sound and popular convention. Like suit counts, however, it is generally overused. In most cases, you or your partner can tell immediately whether or not it is wise to continue with the suit initially led. I recommend that Smith echo be used only in the most obvious situations, i.e. when dummy's solid suit is being run. Otherwise, Smith echo will often be used when it is more important to give partner the count. Here is an example at matchpoints:

```
                    ♠ Axxx
                    ♡ xx
                    ◇ xx
                    ♣ 109876
    ♠ Kx                          ♠ QJ109
    ♡ AQJx          ┌─────────┐   ♡ xxx
    ◇ AQ10x         │ N       │   ◇ K432
    ♣ AKx         W │ W     E │ E ♣ xx
                    │   S     │
                    └─────────┘
                    you
                    ♠ 86x
                    ♡ K10xx
                    ◇ xxx
                    ♣ QJx
```

West	North	East	South
2♣	pass	2◇	pass
2NT	pass	3♣	pass
3♡	pass	3NT	all pass

Opening lead: ♣10

You play the jack of clubs at Trick 1 and West wins with the ace. He now leads the king of spades, which North ducks. Should you begin a Smith echo in spades?

Many will think, "Of course! I want to encourage a club continuation and see no reason to give count in spades." On this deal, however, count is extremely important. If partner incorrectly concludes that you have a doubleton, he should duck the second spade. West will then switch to a heart and make eleven tricks.

On the other hand, if you give partner the spade count, he will win the second spade and continue clubs. Declarer will now cash his four diamonds and two spades, ending up in dummy. At this point, declarer can still get eleven tricks by finessing the heart, but he will be held to nine if it loses! He may well prefer to settle for his ten tricks.

One of my favorite signaling conventions against notrump contracts is a modified version of Foster echo. The original unmodified Foster echo requires that, when unable to beat partner's opening lead or dummy's card, you play your second highest and continue up the line on subsequent tricks in the suit led. The exception is when the ace or king is led. In these cases use a different convention such as ace asks for attitude, king asks for count; also, if the queen is led, play the jack if you have it. Foster echo is described in Amalya Kearse's 1990 edition of *Bridge Conventions Complete* as "a combination count signal and unblocking play", but as originally defined it is an ambiguous count signal. It works quite well whenever your first play is the lowest card outstanding in the suit; partner can infer that you have either a doubleton or a singleton. But suppose you play the six (not the lowest) and then the eight? Did you start with two, three, four, or more cards in the suit? Unless partner holds all or most of the cards lower than the six he will have a hard time knowing. For this reason, Foster echo has properly fallen into disfavor, but I believe it worth resurrecting if modified slightly.

I suggest that you start with your second highest and continue *down the line* on subsequent plays in the suit unless you need to unblock (which rarely happens). By doing so, partner knows you always have one higher in the suit until you are forced to play a higher card than your first one, in which case it is your last. In the example above, if you play the six and then the eight you started with a doubleton. If instead you play the six and then the two, you started with three. If you play the six and then the five, you started with at least three and partner can frequently tell exactly how many by the number of cards lower than the five that he holds in the suit. Furthermore, often partner doesn't really need to know your exact count. Knowing that you still have one higher will usually suffice.

Against suit contracts

Although I have cautioned you against overusing count signals, one situation in which they are clearly necessary is when partner leads a king at Trick 1 and you have to let him know whether or not a ruff is available. We all know to play small from three and start an echo with a doubleton. But what should you play from four small? As far as I know, this is still an unsettled question. I can settle it once and for all.

The best analysis I have seen is, not surprisingly, by Eddie Kantar, though it is not definitive since it lacks thoroughness.[1] He says, "With four small you should play your second highest (some experts play their highest)... I recommend second highest when you can afford it rather than highest or third highest. It usually is clearer... [The] highest card should be reserved to show a doubleton." He disdains third highest, giving an example of where it misleads partner into thinking it was from three small. He concludes, without specifics, that, "If West plays the... second highest, it gives East the best chance to work out the distribution." After doing my own analysis, I have determined that Kantar's conclusions are correct. Although there is no question that having a partnership agreement greatly reduces confusion when you hold four small, the question is, which agreement is best? Let me augment Kantar's arguments with the specific details that he omits.

Playing highest or second highest will rarely mislead partner into thinking you have three small, whereas third highest will do so often. For instance, if you play the 3 from 7-6-3-2, partner will probably play you for the 7-6-3. Since it is far more critical to alert partner that you have an even number as opposed to an odd number than it is to differentiate between four cards versus a doubleton, playing the third highest is inadvisable. On this point Kantar was right on. This is the easy case, however. The trickier one is whether to play highest or second highest, and here Kantar's emphatic conclusion that second highest is best also turns out to be correct, but he fails to provide the analysis. Here it is:

The best approach to this type of question is to case it out, although it may be a laborious process. Let's go through a specific example. Suppose the missing cards from the opening leader's perspective are the 8-7-6-3-2. If you use the rule of the highest card, then (ignoring singletons) if partner plays the 8 it can be from 8-7-6-3, 8-7-6-2, 8-7-3-2, 8-6-3-2, 8-7, 8-6, 8-3, 8-2, whereas if he plays the 7 it can be from 7-6-3-2, 7-6, 7-3, 7-2. So, partner will have started with a doubleton 50% of the time when the 8 appears and 75% of the time when the 7 appears. Alternatively, if you use the rule of the second-highest card, then (again ignoring singletons) if partner

1. "Kantar on Count" in the October 1981 issue of the *Contract Bridge Bulletin*.

plays the 8, it can be from 8-7, 8-6, 8-3, 8-2, whereas if he plays the 7 it can be from 8-7-6-3, 8-7-6-2, 8-7-3-2, 7-6, 7-3, 7-2. So, partner will have started with a doubleton 100% of the time when the 8 appears and 50% of the time when the 7 appears.

So, in this case the strategy of playing the second-highest card, combined with playing partner for a doubleton when the highest outstanding card appears, is best. You will guess right more often than if you play the top card from either holding. Since the numbers remain the same in other examples, second highest will always come out on top. From the above discussion, you can see why the issue has gone unresolved among experts for so long; the reasoning is necessarily subtle. You may have to reread it to understand it fully. Nevertheless, even in these situations, the rule of never giving an unnecessary signal still applies. Consider the following deal:

dummy
- ♠ Ax
- ♡ K42
- ♦ AKQJ109
- ♣ xx

```
      N
  W       E
      S
```

you
- ♠ Qxxxx
- ♡ 53
- ♦ xx
- ♣ 8763

West	North	East	South
	1♣[1]	pass	1♦
2♣	2♦	pass	2♡
pass	4♡	all pass	

1. Strong and artificial.

Opening lead: ♣A

Do not automatically play the club seven followed by the six when partner continues with the queen, even if this happens to be your agreement. If you play the three followed by the six, seven or eight, you know what partner will do. Looking at the dummy, he will switch to a spade (nothing else makes any sense), which is what you want him to do. If you high-low in clubs, however, partner should play you for a doubleton and continue. Here is the complete deal:

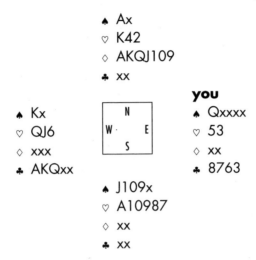

```
                 ♠ Ax
                 ♡ K42
                 ◇ AKQJ109
                 ♣ xx
                                        you
     ♠ Kx                               ♠ Qxxxx
     ♡ QJ6          N                   ♡ 53
     ◇ xxx      W ·     E               ◇ xx
     ♣ AKQxx         S                  ♣ 8763
                 ♠ J109x
                 ♡ A10987
                 ◇ xx
                 ♣ xx
```

As you can see, if you have a doubleton club and no queen of spades, only a club continuation beats the contract, whereas with your actual hand, only a spade shift beats it.

Some experts claim that upside-down carding (UDCA) is superior to standard carding in a very few situations and inferior to it in none. Be that as it may, the improvement is not nearly significant enough to forgo using standard carding if that's what you've grown up with. Old-timers (like me) have played standard carding for decades and our habits are pretty well developed by now. If you are one of us, it is probably not worth the risk, not to mention the effort, to change at this late date. I know several long-time superstars who still play standard carding.

I also highly recommend odd/even discards, or some variant of them, for the simple reason that they conform to the principle of conveying the most information with the fewest number of cards and, as far as I know, they do it in the most effective way. In this method your first discard indicates attitude to the suit discarded: an odd-numbered spot-card encourages — an even one discourages and is also suit-preference.

Trump Management

In one of your earliest bridge lessons you learned that it is a good idea to pull trumps. As you advanced, you discovered that this rule has many exceptions. By the time you neared the end of the course, you probably thought that it was a better idea never to pull trumps! Naturally, the truth lies somewhere in the middle. Each deal is different and you cannot rely on a general rule; you must always apply logic.

The limitless variety of bridge hands requires that you be familiar with different approaches toward managing trumps. Ruffing and crossruffing, reducing trump length to set up a trump coup, endplaying an opponent with the high trump, avoiding a trump tap by discarding a loser, safety-playing to protect against an unacceptable number of trump losers, setting up your suit before pulling trumps in order to maintain control — these are some of the many techniques that you must learn to master.

Do not always be afraid of a ruff by an opponent. Frequently, a ruff will be with a natural trump trick since, if an opponent is short in one suit (the one he is ruffing) he will usually be long in another, namely trumps. As an illustration, consider the following deal, which arose in an open pairs game when I was playing with Steve Sidell:

E-W vul.

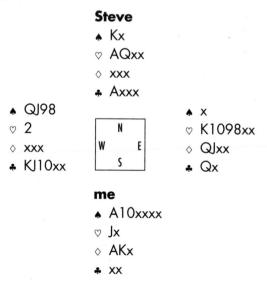

Steve
- ♠ Kx
- ♡ AQxx
- ♢ xxx
- ♣ Axxx

♠ QJ98
♡ 2
♢ xxx
♣ KJ10xx

♠ x
♡ K1098xx
♢ QJxx
♣ Qx

me
- ♠ A10xxxx
- ♡ Jx
- ♢ AKx
- ♣ xx

West	North	East	South
	1♣	1♡	1♠
pass	1NT	pass	3♠
pass	4♠	all pass	

Opening lead: ♡2

Although the heart lead is clearly a singleton, ducking is your only chance to make your contract and it probably won't cost. It will only cost a trick in the event that West has a singleton or doubleton in trumps. If East wins with the king and returns a heart (which he did) instead of a club, you are cold. West ruffs with a natural trump trick and you end up losing only two trumps and a heart after you pitch a club and a diamond on the ♡A-Q. If you win with the ace of hearts, you have no chance to make.

The main reason to pull your opponents' trumps is to limit them to the fewest possible ruffs. At the point in any deal where dummy is out of trumps but the opponents are not, it is generally right to pull trumps as a matter of simple arithmetic; each time you play one, you remove two opposing trump cards but only one of yours. Failure to observe this principle led to one of the most unusual bridge results that I have ever encountered. Playing with Steve Sidell in a regional pairs game, an opponent was playing a contract in a legitimate trump suit (as opposed to, say, a 2-1 fit based on a bidding misunderstanding). The defense took exactly seven tricks. The unprecedented part was that, although neither Steve nor I held a void and the trumps split, all seven defensive tricks were taken in the trump suit! It is hard to conceive how this happened since you would think that one or both of us had to take a trick outside of trumps in order to give partner ruffs. Here is the complete deal:

E-W vul.

```
                ♠ KJxxxx
                ♡ —
                ◇ AK
                ♣ AJ10xx
   me                           Steve
   ♠ 109x          ┌─────────┐   ♠ AQxx
   ♡ J10xx         │    N    │   ♡ AKx
   ◇ x          W  │ W     E │   ◇ 9876x
   ♣ Kxxxx          │    S    │   ♣ x
                 └─────────┘
                ♠ —
                ♡ Q98xxx
                ◇ QJ10xx
                ♣ Qx
```

West	North	East	South
		1◇	1♡
pass	1♠	pass	2♡
pass	2♠	pass	3♡
all pass			

Opening lead: low diamond

Declarer won with the king of diamonds and played the ace. I ruffed and played the ten of spades, ruffed by South. At this point, declarer eschewed the two-for-one rule and led the queen of diamonds. I ruffed and switched to a low club, won by declarer with the queen. Again declarer decided against the rule and played the jack of diamonds. I ruffed again, gave partner a club ruff, and received yet another diamond ruff. At this point, partner claimed his remaining ♡AK. I sincerely believe that exactly seven defensive tricks, all in trumps, with neither defender having a void, without a bidding misunderstanding and with trumps splitting, is a bridge world record.

CHAPTER 3

Bidding Conventions
THE GOOD AND THE BAD

Wh-en you play opposite a new and/or weak partner, the simplest system is best. Avoid convoluted auctions, artificial bids and too many conventions. At the Cavendish I insisted on playing a system that I named WINL, an easy-to-remember acronym pronounced "win-il". It stands for Weak two-bids, Intermediate jump overcalls (defined as an opening bid with a good six-card suit), Non-forcing Stayman, and Limit-raises. If my partner insisted, I also allowed Jacoby transfers. Fortunately, most partners wanted to play them (as did I). All five of these conventions are highly recommended at money bridge. However, by seeming to acquiesce grudgingly to playing transfers, it was easier for me to reject adamantly other less desirable conventions, such as negative doubles, which are superfluous since WINL does not include five-card majors.

After a few sessions, the regulars knew what WINL meant, so that merely saying, "I play WINL" sufficed for any discussion of conventions. Needless to say, neither my partner nor I ever had a bidding disaster caused by forgetting what system we were playing.

Whatever system you finally decide to adopt, treat it as a framework, not a cage. Don't be a slave to your system. It need only be robust enough to cover the most frequent situations. Beyond that, logic will suffice if you merely search for your best available bid, whether or not it perfectly fits all the requirements of your conventions. This deal is taken from a recent regional knockout match. The opponents at our table were Henry Lortz (West) and Dan Jacob:

Helen Abbott

♠ Axx
♡ Jx
♢ QJx
♣ AKxxx

☐

me

♠ KQJ10
♡ Q
♢ xxxx
♣ 1098x

Both vul.

West	North	East	South
	1NT	pass	?

I realized that any contract might be either good or very bad. If partner had four spades, we belonged in spades, maybe even in 4♠ if she had a maximum. If partner had bad hearts, we didn't want to be in notrump, but if she had good hearts and a maximum, we might even want to be in 3NT.

Having no convention that covered all these possibilities (I doubt that there is one), I tried two clubs, over which partner bid two diamonds and I continued with two spades. When opponents asked Helen what this sequence meant, she correctly explained that I showed five spades, four hearts and invitational values, after which she passed with her three spades and a minimum.

After the deal, Henry asked if I had misbid. I said no, explaining that I had merely made my best available bid. Our system provided me with the best solution to my dilemma even though I had to mislead my partner by using a convention without having the agreed-upon holding. If partner had bid spades over two clubs, I'd have raised to three; if partner had bid hearts over two clubs, I'd have bid an invitational two spades. If, on the actual auction, partner had raised my two spade bid to three, I'd have passed. If she had bid three hearts over two spades, showing a maximum with three hearts, I'd have bid 3NT. So, although I had no perfect bid at my disposal, a little logic and the best available bid within our system sufficed to get us to the excellent contract of 2♠, while 1NT has no play.

Against two spades, Henry made the friendly lead of the queen of clubs from QJ doubleton, but nothing was any better. Had he led hearts, I would have merely discarded a diamond on the second one and made the same nine tricks.

It is impossible to devise a perfect system for all possible bridge hands; there are 635,013,559,600 of them! Don't use any convention that makes one bid do too much. It is not necessary that you convey a complete description in one bid. In fact, one bid is usually insufficient to portray most hands adequately. You should strive to have each of your bids narrow your point-count range and/or distribution. A fairly accurate picture will eventually emerge, usually after only one or two additional bids. In a regional knockout match, the same bidding occurred at both tables on the following deal:

Both vul.

Steve Sidell
- ♠ Axx
- ♡ Jx
- ◇ xxxx
- ♣ Jxxx

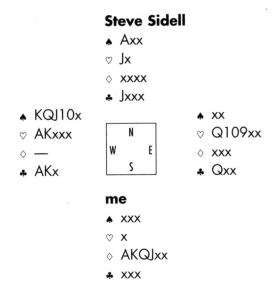

West hand:
- ♠ KQJ10x
- ♡ AKxxx
- ◇ —
- ♣ AKx

East hand:
- ♠ xx
- ♡ Q109xx
- ◇ xxx
- ♣ Qxx

me
- ♠ xxx
- ♡ x
- ◇ AKQJxx
- ♣ xxx

West	North	East	South
	pass	pass	2◇
4◇	pass	4♡	pass

Both our opponents at this table and our teammates at the other table were regular partnerships that had spent many hours honing their bidding system. In fact, our teammates were an excellent, well-seasoned partnership with more than 500 pages of system notes! Their agreements dictate that a jump to four diamonds shows a big hand with both majors whereas a bid of three diamonds asks partner to bid 3NT with diamonds stopped. Both of these are fine conventions; I play them myself. As a result, both West players (being slaves to their systems) dutifully bid four diamonds. After their partners bid four hearts, they both passed, reasoning that they weren't certain that partner had as many as four hearts. Furthermore, they had already shown their hand, so it was up to partner to move.

The given auction violates three of my principles, any one of which, if obeyed, would have sufficed to reach the slam. First, any system is only a framework, which can be broken whenever logic dictates. Second, you should always plan your entire sequence of bids. Third, with a hand this strong, four diamonds tries to do too much with one bid.

A bid of three diamonds followed by a bid of four diamonds if partner bids 3NT is clearly superior to a jump to four diamonds and would have solved both of West's problems. However, neither player was willing to bid three diamonds with this hand because it was anti-system and both thought that the single bid of four diamonds conveyed a complete description.

Had West started by bidding three diamonds (to be followed by four diamonds), partner's (natural) bid of three hearts would have indicated at least a four-card suit with few, if any, wasted values in diamonds. Armed with this knowledge, a subsequent cuebid of clubs by West would be safe at the five-level, even should East merely return to four hearts over four diamonds. On the other hand, if over three diamonds East bids 3NT instead of three hearts, West's subsequent four diamond bid would alert partner that, in addition to having first-round diamond control, West was too strong for an immediate jump to four diamonds.

If West does start with three diamonds followed by four diamonds and then a cuebid of five clubs, facing the possibility that partner might hold a yarborough with four small hearts, East can easily carry on to slam. With East's actual holding, however, he can only muster up a four heart bid over partner's four diamond bid

With the above general principles in mind, let's recap the specific conventions we've already mentioned while also introducing some new ones for discussion. I will exclude the ones about which I am ambivalent.

Old-Fashioned Reverse Drury (Highly Modified)

The original reverse Drury convention specified that a two club bid by a passed hand after partner opens one of a major is artificial and asks opener whether or not his third or fourth seat opening was made with full values; if not, opener merely rebids his suit. Modern reverse Drury also requires trump support for the two club bid. This violates my prohibition against making one bid do too much. The insistence on trump support is both unnecessary and counter-productive. It is unnecessary because you can always show support by either bidding partner's major on your next turn or passing if partner merely rebids his suit. It is counter-productive because by not requiring trump support, a two-club bid can be used fruitfully to launch a description of many other types of hand.

In my version of reverse Drury, two clubs is used as a telling bid, not an asking bid. Responder bids two clubs with *all* maximum passes, where a maximum pass is defined as a hand with good possibilities for game opposite a better than minimum opener with no side suit. It is important to note that any hand with fewer than 11 *good* HCP requires at least two trumps to qualify as a maximum pass. Over two clubs, opener either:

- Rebids two spades with a minimum, which partner should have no qualms about passing with at least two trumps (with fewer than two, he should bid 2NT and expect to have a good chance to make if he has the required 11+ or 12 HCP).

- Bids a new suit other than two diamonds to invite game if partner fits either the new suit or the original major.

- Bids two diamonds to force to game with more than a full opener (with a total of no less than 25 points between you and partner, some game should be available), after which the bidding proceeds naturally.

This approach has the great advantage that whenever a hand is opened in third or fourth seat, all game-forcing sequences begin at the level of two diamonds, providing the maximum bidding room to probe for the best game (frequently 3NT). Furthermore, opener need not waste bidding space by jump shifting over two clubs with a big two-suited hand; he merely starts with two diamonds and follows by bidding his second suit as many times as necessary. An immediate jump shift by opener is now reserved for distributional two-suited hands that are not strong enough to force to game; otherwise, opener would have first bid two diamonds. If partner has a good fit for either suit, he should bid game. If not, he either passes or corrects to opener's first-bid suit to sign off.

Other available responses (besides two clubs) to a third- or fourth-seat major-suit opener are:

- A jump to three clubs with a good weak two-bid in clubs and fewer than two cards in opener's major, after which opener can either force to game by bidding an unmentioned suit, bid 3NT or sign off either by passing or bidding three of his major.

- A non-jump, non-forcing bid at the two-level in any suit other than clubs whenever you have scant support for opener's major with either a good five-card or a broken six-card suit (on most other hands you would have opened with a weak two-bid).

- A natural non-forcing 1NT bid.

- A natural one spade bid over one heart with a non-maximum pass. (With a maximum pass you must begin with two clubs.)

A couple of examples of problem deals in two-over-one that are solved with this version of reverse Drury should suffice to illustrate its advantages.

Suppose you are playing 'modern' reverse Drury. Opener bids one heart and you have a maximum pass with four spades and three hearts. Do you bid one spade or two clubs? If you bid one spade, how do you subsequently show a good hand with three hearts while also staying at the two-level whenever partner next bids 1NT or two of a minor? (A bid at the three-level might be disastrous if partner has a sub-minimum opener.) On the other hand, if you bid two clubs, how do you discover your 4-4-spade fit when opener is 4-5 in the majors? Not only would spades usually play better than hearts, with a double fit you could very well have game if partner has a normal opener opposite your maximum pass.

Using my approach, both problems are solved. You always respond two clubs with a maximum pass. If partner wants to invite game when you fit either hearts or spades, he bids two spades (note: this is not a reverse since he would have bid a game-forcing two diamonds first with the extra values implied by a normal reverse). Now, since partner has shown invitational values and you have a maximum pass, you can safely bid either 2NT or three hearts (with three) if you don't fit spades.

Playing two-over-one, you pick up

♠ x   ♡ Q98xxx   ◇ Axx   ♣ xxx

and the auction proceeds as follows:

West	North	East	South
			pass
pass	1♠	pass	?

Since two hearts would be forcing for one round, you must bid a semi-forcing 1NT. If partner has three hearts and passes, you will be unhappy. On the other hand, if partner bids two spades, what do you do? If you pass, partner may have three hearts; if you bid three hearts, partner may have a singleton heart. All these problems are solved if 1NT and two-level bids like two hearts are non-forcing, showing less than a maximum pass.

Immediate Cuebids by Unpassed Hands

Playing an immediate cuebid by an unpassed hand as always showing a limit raise or better seems unnecessarily restrictive and makes one bid do too much. Just as with Drury, requiring trump support is superfluous since this can be shown on the next bid. An immediate cuebid should be either: (a) a limit raise or better or (b) a game force worth 15+ points including distribution, at least second-round control of an opponent's suit and a strong six-card or better suit. Which hand it is can be clarified at the next turn to bid. In the meantime, opener merely bids as if it were hand (a) until he hears otherwise. If partner has 15+ points, it is unlikely that opener has more than a minimum. Therefore, if the opponents jump to the three- or four-level after a strong cuebid, opener will most likely pass and await partner's next bid.

Some will argue that, without trump support, one can merely bid a new suit to force to game. But, there is a significant difference between a mere game-forcing bid and one showing the equivalent of a strong jump shift. Consider the following pairs of auctions:

(1)	West	North	East	South
				1◇
	1♡	1♠	pass	

	West	North	East	South
				1◇
	1♡	2♡	pass	3◇
	pass	3♠		

The first sequence is a mere one-round force with at least five spades; the second sequence would be game forcing with good spades and slam interest. Note that it is unlikely that North would have slam interest without a useful holding in diamonds.

(2)

West	North	East	South
			1♢
1♡	1♠	3♡	pass
pass	3♠		

West	North	East	South
			1♢
1♡	2♡	3♡	pass
pass	3♠		

The first sequence is not forcing; the second sequence would be game-forcing with good spades and slam interest.

(3)

West	North	East	South
			1♢
1♡	1♠	4♡	pass
pass	4♠		

West	North	East	South
			1♢
1♡	2♡	4♡	pass
pass	4♠		

The first sequence is an opening bid with good spades; the second would be a hand worth 15+ points (including distribution) with good spades and shortness in hearts.

A typical hand for each of the first sequences in the above examples would be

(a) ♠ AQJ10xx ♡ x ♢ Kxx ♣ xxx

A typical hand for each of the second sequences in the above examples would be

(b) ♠ AQJ10xx ♡ x ♢ Kxx ♣ AJx

Try to describe the second hand using standard methods while staying below the five-level. The five-level could easily be too high if partner has a card or two in hearts or the opponents have a diamond ruff available — which is probable on the bidding when an opponent jumps to four hearts (example 3). This is the problem with a generic cuebid that can show a hand as weak as a limit raise. Incidentally, I won't even bother to discuss the more difficult question of how one would bid hands of type (b) if an immediate cuebid were not allowed when the opponents are bidding spades and your suit is hearts.

Puppet Stayman and Four-Way Transfers after an Opening 2NT (or 2♣ and a 2NT Rebid)

Four-way transfers over 1NT is a convention that provides transfer bids for all suits, minors as well as majors. In addition to Jacoby transfers in the majors, a bid of two spades over 1NT transfers to clubs and a bid of 2NT over 1NT transfers to diamonds. To invite 3NT, responder must first use Stayman before bidding 2NT whether or not he is interested in a major suit.

Whereas four-way transfers over 1NT are mainly used to reach the best game or part score, when used over 2NT their primary purpose is to probe for slam. After a 2NT opening:

- A jump to four clubs is Gerber.

- A jump to four diamonds shows a game-forcing 5-5 in the minors, after which opener can bid 4NT to play with stoppers in the majors and an unsuitable hand for slam.

- A jump to four hearts shows 5-5 in the majors with no slam interest.

- A jump to four spades shows 5-5 in the majors with slam interest.

- A bid of three clubs is Puppet Stayman. Since an immediate raise to 3NT is a transfer, you must go through Puppet if you intend to raise to 3NT, even with no interest in a major. This should be alerted.

- Three spades is a transfer to clubs. With a super-fit in clubs (x-x-x-x, Q-x-x, or better), opener bids 3NT (instead of four clubs), after which partner can either pass, bid four or five clubs to sign off or make a short-suit slam try which partner can reject by rebidding notrump with wasted values or accept by bidding another suit (which would be natural). With no super-fit, suit bids other than clubs by responder show a stopper in the suit; opener bids naturally.

- 3NT is a transfer to diamonds. With a super-fit in diamonds (x-x-x-x, Q-x-x, or better), opener bids four clubs (instead of four diamonds), after which partner can either correct to 4NT, bid four or five diamonds to sign off or make a short-suit slam try, which partner can reject by rebidding notrump with wasted values or accept by bidding another suit (which would be natural). With no super-fit, suit bids other than diamonds by responder show a stopper in the suit; opener bids naturally.

Suppose partner opens 2NT and you hold:

♠ x ♡ Kx ◇ KJ10xxx ♣ QJxx.

If partner holds wastage in spades (he may even have five of them) you want to play notrump. If partner has no spade wastage without good clubs you want to play five diamonds if he doesn't fit diamonds (less than Q-x-x) and six if he does. If partner has no spade wastage with good clubs you want to play five clubs if he has no diamond honor and six if he does. Playing four-way transfers you can find out everything by starting with 3NT. If opener bids:

(a) Four clubs showing good diamonds (Qxx or better), you bid four spades (your short suit) and if opener now bids 4NT you pass; if he bids five clubs (natural) you bid six clubs and if he bids anything else you bid six diamonds, since opener has little if any waste in spades.

(b) Four diamonds showing weak diamonds (less than three to the queen), you bid four hearts showing a stopper and pass if opener now bids 4NT. If he bids four spades (natural), you bid 4NT showing a club stopper; if he bids five clubs (natural) you raise to six since partner would have bid 4NT with clubs and good spades so you can infer that he probably has a diamond honor.

I am obligated to mention one disadvantage of playing this convention — going through Puppet Stayman on the way to 3NT gives opponents extra information. Although this is a substantial drawback, I still feel that the positives outweigh it. Also, don't open 2NT with five spades and four hearts since you will be unable to find a 4-4 heart fit.

Singleton-Showing Bids (i.e. Splinters)

These bids are unusually high jumps in a new suit and show strength with a small singleton in the suit bid plus good trump support for partner. Their value is indisputable. Knowing whether or not you have duplication opposite a singleton is crucial for effective slam bidding. Furthermore, reserving a double jump shift for this purpose gives up little. I believe that of all the modern conventions, splinters provide the best argument against Simon's position and to a large extent my own. In *Design for Bidding*, Simon asserts that "There is not and there never can be an absolutely accurate system of bidding". He presents the following example to illustrate his statement and highlight the futility of trying to solve the problem of duplication of values:

HAND 1

West		**East**	
♠	AJxxxx	♠	KQ10xx
♡	KQJx	♡	x
◊	Qx	◊	A10x
♣	x	♣	KQJx

HAND 2

West		**East**	
♠	Axxxxx	♠	Kxxxx
♡	xxxx	♡	x
◊	xx	◊	Axx
♣	x	♣	xxxx

Simon says that with Hand 1 there is clearly "no difficulty in reaching four spades and perhaps making five." No argument there. He goes on to say that, with Hand 2, "Four spades is still on ice. But just try and bid it without help from the opponents." Again, no argument. But singleton-showing bids, such as splinters, certainly improve the odds of reaching makeable games or slams on many hands that are between the extremes of Hand 1 and Hand 2. Here is an example:

West	**East**
♠ AQxxx	♠ KJxxx
♡ Ax	♡ Qxx
◇ xxxx	◇ x
♣ Kx	♣ AQxx

Playing splinters, East responds four diamonds to West's one spade opening to show diamond shortness and good spades. West has the perfect diamond holding to explore for slam, namely no wasted strength in the suit (all honors other than the ace would be wasted opposite a small singleton). Using our cuebidding methods, West now bids four hearts, East bids five clubs and slam is easily reached with a total of only 25 combined points.

Lebensohl after Doubles of Weak Two-Bids

Lebensohl reserves the bid of 2NT after partner doubles a weak two-bid to show a weak hand. Any other bid shows values and invites game. After two notrump, the doubler bids three clubs with any hand that isn't strong enough to invite game opposite known weakness and passes partner's subsequent bid. Lebensohl greatly reduces the preemptive effectiveness of weak two-bids, though nothing can diminish their lead-directing power. Some method of applying the brakes is needed in order to stay out of bad games. Without Lebensohl (or some other similar convention), how can partner know the difference between a weak or an invitational three-heart response to his takeout double of two spades? Suppose the bidding has gone:

West	North	East	South
2♠	dbl	pass	3♡
pass	?		

If you, as South, hold

♠ xx ♡ Qxxxx ◇ xxx ♣ Jxx

you want partner to pass. But if you hold

♠ xx ♡ KQxxx ◇ xxx ♣ Axx

you want partner to bid four with extras. If partner guesses wrong in either situation, it will result in a big swing against you. Playing Lebensohl, South bids 2NT with the first hand and then bids three hearts over partner's three clubs to show weakness with hearts.

Two Diamonds Semi-Automatic after a Two-Club Opener

I include this convention to discourage those who wish to bid a suit to show two of the top three honors. Note: control-showing bids or the use of two hearts as a super-negative are not discouraged. The biggest problem with showing two of the top three honors is that it unnecessarily complicates the bidding when opener has a balanced hand (especially with a five-card major). How does partner know how good your suit really is? And with a balanced hand, knowing you will be in charge of placing the contract, does he even care? If he is balanced, should he rebid 2NT or raise with three-card trump support? If 2NT, does Puppet Stayman still apply? Do four-way transfers still apply? If not, how do you subsequently describe 5-5 or 5-4 hands? Furthermore, even if you solve these problems when partner is balanced, your bid will have gained little and will potentially cost you valuable bidding space whenever partner has a one-suited or two-suited hand. For example:

♠ A
♡ AKQJxxx
◊ AQx
♣ xx

you
♠ KQJxx
♡ x
◊ J10x
♣ xxxx

West	North	East	South
	2♣	pass	2♠
pass	3♡	pass	?

Even if you manage to solve your rebid problem somehow, you will still have lost a level of bidding and, on this deal, partner is much more interested in finding out things other than whether you have two of the top three honors in spades. If you start with two diamonds, however, you have an easy two spade bid over two hearts while leaving room for partner to bid 2NT, three clubs, three diamonds or three hearts.

The bid of a natural suit should be reserved for a suit that rates to be as good as partner's if he had opened two clubs with a strong suit of his own. This provides a choice of suits in which to play the deal. If partner prefers your suit, he can raise immediately and a cuebidding sequence can be initiated at a low level if slam is a consideration. Moreover, he usually will prefer your suit if he holds a modicum of support since, as trumps, it becomes a fruitful source of entries into the weaker hand.

Besides, you can still show a suit with two of the top three honors by starting with two diamonds and then bidding your suit. Now your partner knows you are likely to have as little as K-Q-x-x-x, since with K-Q-J-x-x-x you would have bid them immediately. Furthermore, your partner has other tools at his disposal if he really needs to know about two of the top three honors (notably RKC Blackwood or the grand slam force).

Ace and King Cuebids

In addition to other advantages, this treatment increases the effectiveness of, and eliminates a few potential problems with, the recommended cuebidding approach. With ace and king cuebids, a cuebid is defined as showing first- or second-round control. Once a cuebidding sequence has been initiated, you start with your lowest-ranking cuebid, whether it be an ace, king, singleton or void. This method warns partner to stop probing for slam and sign off in game if he too has neither first- nor second-round control of a bypassed suit (you are clearly off the first two tricks in the suit). If you cuebid the same suit twice, you show first- *and* second-round control; however, you shouldn't do this unless you have already bid all other suits of which you have first- or second-round control and there is still enough bidding room available. Consider the following example:

West	East
♠ Qxx	♠ —
♡ AQxxx	♡ KJ10xx
◇ QJxxx	◇ AKxx
♣ —	♣ Qxxx

Using Ace and King Cuebids the auction would proceed as follows:

West	North	East	South
		1♡	pass
2◇ [1]	pass	3◇	pass
3♡	pass	3♠	pass
4♣	pass	4◇	pass
5♣	pass	5◇	pass
5♡	pass	5♠	pass
7♡	all pass		

1. GF.

A very nice spot with only 24 combined points! West's three heart bid sets the trump suit. East's three spade bid shows first- or second-round control as do West's four club bid and East's four diamond bid. West's five club bid shows first- and second-round control as do East's bids of five diamonds and five spades. At this point, West has an easy seven heart bid since East's five spade bid forces slam and shows grand slam interest, which he could not do with a jack high trump suit. Try finding this grand slam without effective cuebidding, for instance if either side uses Blackwood!

Note that this convention conforms to the principle of not making one bid do too much. Remember, a cuebid suggests extra values, but if your cuebids are restricted to first-round controls, you can find yourself with no sensible bid on a hand with extras if you have no aces or voids.

Four-Card Majors

Systems using four-card majors are more natural than those using five-card majors and they also have the added advantage of not requiring negative doubles at any level. Even if you are uncomfortable with the idea of playing four-card majors, I strongly recommend that you play them for a while in order to get practice playing in 4-3 fits.[1] You will discover that as long as the dummy has a useful doubleton with three trumps and trumps split no worse than 4-2, these hands play quite well and are often your best contract. Partner should not hesitate to raise with this holding (i.e. three trumps and a side doubleton), even in competition if his doubleton is in the opponent's suit, as is usually the case. Keep this in mind when we discuss support doubles.

When playing four-card majors there are two schools of thought as to what to open when holding two roughly equal four-card majors. Opening one spade provides you with a more convenient rebid whereas opening one heart leaves partner room to bid one spade and, if he doesn't, you can forget about bidding your spade suit. I prefer the second approach, but admittedly it is harder to handle if the opponents overcall at the two-level. If one of your four-card majors is significantly better than the other, open in the stronger suit for lead directing purposes.

Strangely enough, some advocates of five-card majors recommend the following inconsistency. While they continue to forfeit the advantages of penalty doubles at the one-level in order to ensure that they won't miss a 4-4 major-suit fit, whenever partner responds one heart to their opening bid of one club, they prefer to rebid 1NT rather than one spade with four of them! So, they are quite comfortable missing their 4-4 spade fit whenever partner is 4-4 in the majors with a hand too weak to bid again over 1NT. Furthermore, suppose partner has the wrong shape to pass 1NT. If he holds five hearts and four spades with a weak hand, what does he do? What if he is

---

1. Also known as Moysian fits, after Alphonse (Sonny) Moyse who was a great proponent of them.

4-4-1-4? These seem like unsolvable problems unless you introduce additional artificial bids, which have drawbacks of their own. On the other hand, I have yet to discover any substantial advantages to compensate for these problems.

Strong Jump Shifts vs. Weak Jump Shifts

At matchpoints, as opposed to money bridge or IMPs, good slam bidding is less important and preemption more so; I am therefore ambivalent as to whether to prefer weak jump shifts or strong jump shifts. However, I *do* advocate strong jump shifts over weak ones when not playing matchpoints, even in two-over-one systems. Two-over-one bidders who play weak jump shifts will argue that strong jump shifts are superfluous, since a bid at the two-level is game forcing. Furthermore, won't a strong jump shift use up valuable cuebidding space in any system? Although both objections have some merit, the advantages of strong jump shifts over weak ones outweigh the disadvantages.

To answer the first objection, there is a significant difference between a mere game-forcing bid and one showing 17+ points. Using a simple two-level response for both kinds of hand makes one bid do too much. Other jump shifts such as Bergen, mini-splinters, fit-showing jumps, etc. are also frequently used to narrow the ambiguity of a game-forcing two-over-one bid. The relative merits of these bids vis-à-vis strong or weak jump shifts are not being considered here.

As to the second objection, the information conveyed amply compensates for the lost bidding room. If you start with a mere two-level bid on a powerhouse, you will have a hard time showing the real strength of your hand. However, if you make a strong jump shift, partner will, with many hands, know enough to start cooperating immediately with cuebids rather than misjudging that his hand is unsuited for slam. If so, you will regain the lost bidding space since partner won't waste a level to show you a minimum if, in fact, he doesn't have one in light of your jump shift. Also, he can safely raise your suit with as little as Q-x, again setting the stage for immediate cuebidding. Example:

West		East	
♠ KQ10xx		♠ Jx	
♡ AJx		♡ KQx	
◇ Qx		◇ AKxxxxx	
♣ Q10x		♣ A	

Using strong jump shifts the auction proceeds

West	North	East	South
1♠	pass	3◇	pass
4◇	pass	4♡	pass
4♠	pass	5♣	pass
5♡	pass	6♣	pass
6◇	all pass		

A fine spot which makes whenever there is no spade ruff available and the diamonds are not 4-0. Note that West should bid four diamonds as opposed to 3NT since partner's jump shift is predicated on 17+ points and either very good diamonds or spade support. In either case showing the queen of diamonds is more important than showing a partial club stopper and, after partner shows the king of hearts, opener's hand is now worth a four spade cuebid on the way to five diamonds.

Without strong jump shifts the auction is likely to go:

West	North	East	South
1♠	pass	2◇	pass
2NT	pass	3◇	pass
3NT	pass	?	

East has a choice of bids. If he thinks partner has a singleton diamond he should pass. If he is feeling aggressive, he might venture 4NT in which case West should bid six diamonds and all will be well. Note that 6NT has no play with a club lead.

Support Doubles and Redoubles

Low-level penalty doubles are far too valuable to be lightly abandoned for other purposes, such as to show three- as opposed to four-card trump support (known as a support double) in order to apply the flawed 'law' of total tricks. The utility of an extra trump is marginal. If you have three-card trump support for partner with a doubleton in the overcalled suit, as is usually the case, you can safely raise, but you would regret not being able to make a penalty double if you held a defensive hand, had length in the opponent's suit and were short in partner's suit. True, partner may reopen with a double for you if you pass, but suppose he doesn't? This is the same problem you run into with negative doubles.

Consider the following deal. You hold:

♠ AKJx   ♡ x   ◇ AKx   ♣ AJxxx

E-W vul.

West	North	East	South
			1♣
pass	1♡	1♠	?

The inability to make a penalty double on this kind of hand is too steep a price to pay for the dubious value of differentiating between three and four trumps. Incidentally, this is the companion hand to the first one in Patience is a Virtue in Chapter 2.

Along the same lines, use a redouble to show a good defensive hand instead of three-card support for partner:

♠ AKJx   ♡ x   ◇ AKx   ♣ AJxxx

West	North	East	South
			1♣
pass	1♡	dbl	redbl

High-Level Negative Doubles

If you play four-card majors, negative doubles are unnecessary at any level and should be avoided so that you can more easily penalize the opponents at low levels. If you play five-card majors, I recommend that negative doubles be played through the two-level only, and be 'card-showing' above that. The difference between the two is that a 'card-showing' double does not guarantee four cards in the unbid major whereas a negative double does. If your side has the preponderance of strength and the opponents bid at the three-level, chances are that the 4-4 major-suit fit that you might miss if you don't play negative doubles will not split 3-2; you will be better off in the long run taking your sure profit (usually a large one). Furthermore, your partner is permitted to bid a four-card major after a card-showing double if his hand is not suitable for defense.

I am further persuaded to abandon high-level negative doubles after having read *Contested Auctions*, a book by Mike Lawrence in which he advocates negative doubles. At various points in the book, he discusses bidding problems that he maintains have no easy solution, whereas each of them is only a problem if you are playing negative doubles at the three-level, a fact that he fails to mention. The problems all center around hands where you have some values without length in the unbid major, in which case you frequently have to pass and let the opponents buy it undoubled.

Systems-On When Opponent Makes a Penalty Double of 1NT

Playing systems-on in this situation has one glaring weakness with little return compensation, namely that you lose the ability to run from 1NT doubled to two clubs whenever you have clubs. Holding clubs should be a blessing when 1NT gets doubled and you are weak, but playing systems-on converts it to a curse.

To begin with, two clubs is the safest place to start running inasmuch as it encourages doubler's partner to bid since he can do so at the two-level with any suit other than clubs. It also leaves room for partner to pull two clubs doubled to any five-card suit he may hold. Furthermore, transferring play to partner after his 1NT opener is doubled for penalty in the immediate seat will be *disadvantageous* whenever the double is based on a long strong suit. The doubler's partner might not lead it whereas the doubler certainly will. I recommend the following approach when your partner's 1NT gets doubled for penalty:

- You (not partner) *must* run if you can't stand the double. (It is harder for opponents to make, and sit for, a double of a two-level suit contract than to defend 1NT doubled.) With suits of equal length, start with the lowest. Although both you and your partner will need to depend on your psychological skills whenever deciding whether or not to pull a double (especially if you are not dealt a five-card suit), you are no better off playing systems-on.

- If you pass, you show a willingness to play 1NT doubled and partner can either pass with a minimum or redouble with a maximum.

- If you redouble, the opponents have erred and will pay for it.

For example, suppose you hold a 3-2-4-4 yarborough and partner's opening 1NT is doubled for penalties. Playing systems-on, you must pass and take your lumps. With my approach, you bid two clubs and avoid a large penalty whenever two clubs doesn't get doubled, as is often the case. In particular, if the original doubler was counting on running a long suit against 1NT, it will be virtually impossible for him to sit for partner's double of two clubs. Moreover, you will be better off in two clubs doubled than 1NT doubled whenever partner holds clubs. Even if he doesn't, he may pull to his own suit or another one of yours (in this case, diamonds).

Negative Doubles after a 1NT Opener

The most potent effect of any 1NT opener is that opponents enter the auction at severe risk. If your partner has 5 to 9 points with four (or sometimes only three) trumps, he will double and you will collect a nice profit 90% of the time. If you play negative doubles, however, you lose this advantage. I recommend that all doubles of real suits by opponents be for penalty after a 1NT opener (or overcall) by your side. If you are strong enough to probe for game with one or more four-card majors, you can cuebid or use Lebensohl (in which any bid but 2NT after an overcall is invitational to game). With a weaker hand you may miss a 4-4 major fit, but only a partscore is at stake, which is not enough compensation for losing the ability to make penalty doubles when warranted.

On the other hand, playing negative doubles over *artificial* overcalls is a good idea. It allows you either to compete for a partscore with a weak hand (by making a negative double) or to make a penalty double (by passing and then doubling). Incidentally, when in doubt, the double of an artificial suit shows that suit (unless you have agreed otherwise, in which case you would not be in doubt).

Hamilton (Cappelletti) over 1NT Openers

The Hamilton convention over a 1NT opener uses two clubs to show any one-suited hand, two diamonds to show both majors, two hearts to show hearts and a minor, two spades to show spades and a minor, 2NT to show both minors, and double for penalty. The problem with Hamilton is that you unnecessarily lose the preemptive value of a direct *natural* one-suited two heart or two spade bid. There are several modified versions of Hamilton (as well as other conventional bids over 1NT) that preserve the natural major-suit overcall while still covering all two-suited hands. These are to be preferred.

The convention I recommend over an opponent's 1NT opener is:

- 2♣ shows either a one-suited hand in a minor or a two-suited hand with a major and a minor. Over 2♣ partner must bid 2◇ unless he has a one-suited hand of his own, in which case he either bids it or passes (if it's clubs). After a two-diamond response, if the 2♣ bidder has:

- a one-suited minor, he passes if it's diamonds and bids 3♣ if it's clubs.

- a two-suited hand with a major and a minor, he bids his major. Partner can then either pass if he likes the major or bid 2NT to ask what the minor is.

- 2◇ shows both majors.

- 2♡ shows hearts.

- 2♠ shows spades.

- 2NT shows both minors.

- Double is for penalty.

Principle of Fast Arrival (PFA)

The Principle of Fast Arrival unwisely wastes valuable bidding space. In fact, a principle of *slow* arrival (hereafter dubbed PSA) is superior in all game-forcing auctions. Let's look at two examples:

(1) Suppose you are playing Jacoby 2NT and you open one of a major with no singleton. If your partner bids 2NT, the PFA dictates that you jump to four of your major with a minimum and bid three only if you have extras. Why you should ever do this is beyond me. You can always bid three and then four (without cuebidding) to show a minimum. But, since the 2NT bidder's hand is unlimited — unless, unlike most tournament players, you also happen to be playing strong jump shifts (which, as I have already mentioned, are preferable to weak ones at money bridge or IMPs) — why jump to four and deprive him of cuebidding space whenever he is interested in a slam opposite even a minimum opener? In any game-forcing sequence, an immediate jump in your opening suit should be used only to show solid trumps.

(2) Suppose you play two-over-one and the auction has proceeded:

West	East
1♠	2♦
2♠	?

The opponents passed throughout. Playing the PFA, a bid of four spades would be weaker than a bid of three spades followed by four spades. Is there any rational reason for doing this? It is certainly plausible that, even though you have a minimum for your nonetheless *game-forcing* bid, opener might still be interested in slam once you show support. Now what can he do? He would have to make a unilateral decision as to whether or not to start probing for slam beyond the game level, whereas if you play the PSA, he could probe while staying a level lower.

The 1NT Balancing Bid

When you are in the passout seat after an opposing one bid, 1NT should be reserved for a balanced hand with 10 to at most 14 points. With 10 or 11, don't reopen over one club, since partner would have bid immediately unless he has clubs or a hand that is too weak for a one-level overcall in *any* suit. I recommend that reopening bids follow this scheme:

- Bid one of a suit or 1NT with any hand that is less than an opener.

- With a mere opening bid, jump if you hold a five-card or longer suit. Otherwise, double so that partner can happily pass if the main reason he didn't overcall was that he had opener's suit.

- With more than a minimum opening bid, start with either a double or a cuebid. If you wish, you can play a reopening 1NT as 10 to 13+ points, and an immediate jump to 2NT in the balancing seat as 18 or more in order to cover the complete spectrum of ranges with balanced hands. You would then treat double followed by a bid of notrump as a 1NT opener (14+ to 17).

This approach carries the extremely valuable advantage of being able to tell immediately whether or not the reopener has a good hand.

Multi Two-Diamond Bids

The Multi two-diamond bid has only recently caught on in the States and many of its variations are still disallowed in most U.S. tournaments. However, it is widely used abroad. There are many versions of Multi, but they all include the use of a two diamond opening to show a weak two-bid in *either* major. It has been estimated that there are 64 different flavors of Multi currently in use, so be sure you have thoroughly discussed what you mean by Multi before agreeing to play it with a new partner. A commonplace variation is to enlarge the meaning of a two-diamond opener so that it also includes strong balanced hands.

With a weak hand, whichever Multi variation is played, responder bids two hearts over two diamonds to ask for clarification. In simple Multi, opener will either pass two hearts or bid two spades (in more complex versions, opener may also bid 2NT to show a strong balanced hand). With a stronger hand responder still bids two hearts if he has no interest in a heart game, but raises spades with game interest in spades (or bids game directly) if opener bids two spades over two hearts. On the other hand, if responder has game interest only in hearts, he bids two spades over two diamonds. Opener then passes with spades and bids three or four hearts with hearts. With game interest in either major, responder bids 2NT and opener bids three clubs with a heart minimum, three diamonds with a heart maximum, three hearts with a spade minimum, three spades with a spade maximum. If the two diamond bid is overcalled, an immediate cuebid is GF and asks opener to clarify, while a double is takeout. In and of themselves, these are small compensation, if any, for the loss of a weak two diamond bid.

Moreover, the disadvantage of sometimes having to guess which suit partner holds is significant and occurs quite frequently in competition.

Here is an example :

N-S vul.

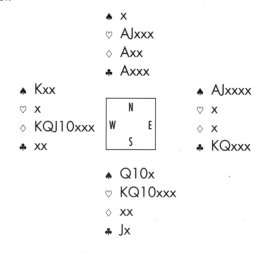

```
                    ♠ x
                    ♡ AJxxx
                    ◇ Axx
                    ♣ Axxx
   ♠ Kxx                            ♠ AJxxxx
   ♡ x           ┌─────────┐        ♡ x
   ◇ KQJ10xxx    │    N    │        ◇ x
   ♣ xx          │ W     E │        ♣ KQxxx
                 │    S    │
                 └─────────┘
                    ♠ Q10x
                    ♡ KQ10xxx
                    ◇ xx
                    ♣ Jx
```

West	North	East	South
			2◇
3◇	?		

North-South are cold for a heart game and North would bid it if he knew his partner had hearts. Furthermore, even if East-West find their four spades save then North-South will still get +100 (or +200 if North doubles). But North must pass, in case partner holds spades, and let the opponents peacefully make at least +110 in three diamonds.

Nevertheless, Multi is a useful convention. Why? Because it frees up the opening bids of two of a major for other uses. There are plenty of options. Some play that an opening bid of two of a major shows a hand in the upper range of a weak two-bid whereas two diamonds shows a weaker hand. Others use two hearts as Flannery (a minimum opener with four spades and five hearts) and two spades as a minor two-suiter. My personal choice is to use bids of two of a major to show weak two-suited hands with the bid major and an unspecified minor. These are called Polish two-bids and unfortunately are also disallowed at many U.S. tournaments. The advantage of Polish two-bids is that these hands can be hard to handle in competitive auctions without them.

Two-Way New Minor Forcing (NMF)

Both one-way NMF (recommended, if modified) and two-way NMF (not recommended) arise when partner bids one of a major over your opening bid of one of a minor and you rebid 1NT. The conventions both require that the bid of a new minor suit is artificial and forcing for at least one round. The main difference between them is that in two-way NMF, the bid of *either* minor is artificial and forcing (note that two-way NMF is a misnomer since responder's two-level minor-suit bid may not be new!), whereas in one-way NMF only the bid of the *new* minor is artificial and forcing. In two-way NMF a bid of two clubs is invitational and a bid of two diamonds is game-forcing. In the conventional one-way NMF, the bid of the new minor is invitational.

Although both versions of NMF disallow the introduction of a natural new minor, two-way NMF also precludes the possibility of showing support for partner's minor at the two-level. This loss violates the rule of showing support with weak hands at the earliest convenient level so as to be able to sit for a penalty double. Furthermore, one-way NMF is adequate to cover all situations that two-way NMF does (as long as opener always rebids one spade over one heart with four spades!) provided that: (1) the opener's first responsibility is to show three-card support for responder's major; (2) you do not need invitational values to use it. Responder merely jumps to the three-level over 1NT on all game-forcing hands (rather than wasting time by first bidding two diamonds if you are playing two-way NMF). Requiring that one must have an invitational hand to use one-way NMF is unnecessarily restrictive and requires one bid to do too much. If the bidder of the new minor wants to invite, he merely does so at his next turn.

Let's look at some examples. Suppose the bidding has gone:

West	North	East	South
			1♣
pass	1♠	pass	1NT
pass	?		

North holds

♠ QJxxx   ♡ Kxx   ◊ x   ♣ Jxxx

In one-way NMF, North bids two clubs to show club support, and on deals where South holds three spades, he can bid two spades; with a doubleton spade, he can pass. In two-way NMF, North also bids two clubs. Now, however, his minor-suit holdings are completely unknown and opener can't pass. You must play clubs at the three-level. Furthermore, if the opponents enter the auction over two clubs, there is no way for opener to know what to do. He might want to double if he knows partner is short in clubs, or he might want to compete in clubs if he knows partner has length. Alternatively, he might want to defend peacefully. Thus you have an unsolvable dilemma. Moreover, if opener does double, then partner will have to pull if he has unannounced club support (according to my rule); but if opener has three small clubs, then this would be the wrong action.

Suppose North holds five spades and four hearts. With a weak hand, he merely bids two hearts over 1NT in both one-way and two-way NMF. With an invitational hand, he uses one-way NMF by bidding two diamonds and then bids hearts at his next opportunity. With a game-forcing hand, he bypasses NMF and bids three hearts over 1NT.

West	North	East	South
			1♣
pass	1♠	pass	1NT
pass	?		

Now suppose North holds

♠ QJxxx   ♡ Kxx   ◊ Jxxx   ♣ x

He should bid two diamonds, planning to pass whatever partner bids. Opener should not jump to three spades to show a maximum with three spades, nor should he jump to three hearts with four hearts, two spades and a maximum. Doing so will only get him too high when partner has no interest in game. Again, partner can always raise if he wants to invite game.

This hand illustrates why opener's first responsibility should be to show three-card support for partner. Many play that opener's first responsibility is to show four hearts, but this example shows why this is misguided. If opener bids two hearts over two diamonds with three-card spade support, what does responder do now with this hand? His choices are pass, 2NT and three diamonds, but now he will either play spades at the three-level rather than the two-level or play in two hearts in his 4-3 fit rather than two spades in his 5-3 fit. True, using this method North may end up playing two spades in a 5-3 fit rather than two hearts in a 4-4 fit, but this is usually inferior only when considering the best game or slam.

Fourth Suit Forcing to Game

This convention states that when opener and responder have started the bidding with four consecutive new suits, they are forced to game. Without modification, the convention is again overly restrictive. This is my last example of making one bid do too much. The convention should be modified as follows:

(1) The following auction is a one-round force only and not game forcing.

West	North	East	South
	1♣	pass	1◊
pass	1♡	pass	1♠

To force to game with four spades, jump to two spades over one heart.

(2) When the bidding has begun with four consecutive suits, it is forcing for one round only, and becomes game forcing *only if* responder does not rebid the fourth suit at his next turn. If he does rebid the fourth suit, it shows an *invitational* hand with ten or more cards in the two suits he has bid (exception: if opener bids notrump after the fourth suit by responder, then the rebid of the fourth suit *is* game forcing, since you can get out with a pass if you want to).

Let's explore the advantages of this approach. To begin with, nothing is lost, since the hands on which you want to play fourth suit game forcing are all hands where you have a fit for opener or an independent major of your own. In that case, you can support partner or rebid your major after bidding the fourth suit and it *will* be game forcing. However, look what happens if you don't have either of those hands, i.e. you have an invitational two-suiter in the other two suits. These hands are unmanageable in two-over-one if you play fourth suit game forcing. Some try to handle them by playing that a *jump* into the fourth suit by responder shows these types of hands. If your second suit is clubs, however, you will sometimes have to jump to the four-level, which bypasses 3NT. With my approach, you stay at the three-level. Also, you can now play the jump into the fourth suit as something else (I recommend that it be a mini-splinter in support of opener's second suit). Here are some illustrative examples:

You hold:

♠ AJ10xx ♡ KQxxx ◇ x ♣ xx

Partner opens one diamond, you bid one spade and partner bids two clubs. Do you really want to play two hearts as game forcing? I think you would much rather play two hearts, followed by three hearts, as an invitational 5-5 if partner doesn't rebid 2NT over two hearts.

You hold:

♠ KJ10xx ♡ x ◇ x ♣ AQxxxx

Partner opens one heart, you bid one spade (playing two-over-one, you can't bid two clubs; it's game forcing!) and partner bids two diamonds. Now what? This is a difficult hand, but your best option is to bid a non-game forcing three clubs and then decide what to do over partner's bid. You can still get out below game by next bidding a non-forcing four clubs if partner either rebids one of his suits or takes a spade preference. In all these cases, partner's hand is unlimited and you owe him another bid (since from his perspective, your three club bid could have been artificial and GF). By bidding four clubs, you alert partner that this was not the case and that he is now in charge of placing the final contract, armed with the knowledge that you have an invitational two-suiter. If partner raises three clubs to four, you must bid five (since, as before, his hand is unlimited), but you are happy to do so having found a fit.

You hold:

♠ KJ10xx ♡ x ◇ AQxxx ♣ xx

Partner opens one heart, you bid one spade partner bids two clubs, you bid two diamonds, and partner bids 2NT. This is a non-forcing auction and you should pass. If you have game interest (with a better hand than the one given) you can bid three diamonds, which is now forcing since you would have passed 2NT if you wanted to play below game. Partner's 2NT bid shows a minimum hand. With more, partner must bid anything other than 2NT, such as 3NT or two hearts, two spades, three clubs, or three diamonds, all of which are forcing bids.

Namyats

Namyats is a convention that uses opening bids of four clubs and four diamonds to show strong preempts in hearts and spades respectively. With the right agreements in place, it can become a useful constructive slam bidding tool, while discouraging partner from being too optimistic after a (weaker) four hearts or four spades opening bid. I like Namyats, but not so much as to recommend it strongly. I have included it here for two reasons, neither of which is particular pertinent to the themes of this book. The first is to inform those of you who don't already know or haven't yet bothered to figure it out that the derivation of this convention's weird-sounding name is 'Stayman' spelled backwards.

The second reason, since this is the end of the book, is to tell you an amusing story, so as to follow the old adage, "Always leave them laughing". I believe it involves another bridge world record, in which Namyats plays a prominent role. In a sixteen-board team match at the Seattle regional, my partner, Mike Wilson, and I went to compare results with our teammates at the halfway point. As occasionally happens, we were tied, but astonishingly enough, this had occurred because the scores on every deal were identical at the two tables! This came to the attention of one of the directors, Mike Roberts, who remarked that it had probably happened before, although he had never seen it. Nevertheless, he was intrigued enough to see if the phenomenon would continue. We were all pretty sure that a ninth consecutive identical result without a passout would set the record, whereupon I, sitting South, picked up:

♠ QJ10xx　♡ KJ10x　◇ xx　♣ Ax

Both vul.

West	North	East	South
	3NT*	all pass	

When asked to explain my alert, I said we were playing Namyats and 3NT was a transfer to four clubs showing a four-level preempt in an unspecified minor. After I passed, everybody was somewhat surprised. When they had settled down, West also passed.

I reasoned that partner's suit was probably diamonds and if so 3NT should be a reasonable spot. When the dummy was tabled, Mike had a look of utter disappointment — his suit was clubs! The opponents reeled off the first ten tricks consisting of the ♠A-K, the ace of hearts and seven diamonds. When the debacle ended, partner remarked, "So much for the world record." To which I replied, "Not so fast."

I realized that the score could still be tied if our partners reached and made exactly five diamonds. They would score +600 for their game and we had scored -600 for 3NT down six. Sure enough, as fate would have it, that is exactly what happened! Our streak ended on the next board, but I believe that the bridge gods allowed this freak result at that exact moment for the sole purpose of giving us the world record. This was the complete deal:

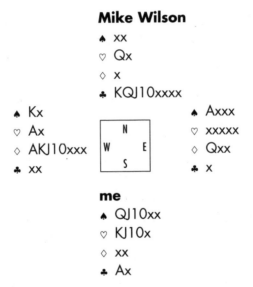

Mike Wilson

♠ xx
♡ Qx
◇ x
♣ KQJ10xxxx

West:
♠ Kx
♡ Ax
◇ AKJ10xxx
♣ xx

East:
♠ Axxx
♡ xxxxx
◇ Qxx
♣ x

me
♠ QJ10xx
♡ KJ10x
◇ xx
♣ Ax

Opening lead: low heart

At the other table this was the auction:

West	North	East	South
	4♣	pass	pass
4◇	pass	5◇	all pass

Opening lead: ♣K

Afterword

Although this book is short by modern standards, I refuse to lengthen it by adding filler. I believe that quality is more important than quantity and that the quality of my book would suffer if I included tips that I am lukewarm about. This book is neither a thorough treatise on a given aspect of the game, nor a rehash of previous territory that has already been adequately covered by others, nor a compendium of humorous deals. It is a presentation of fresh viewpoints. As such it is *a priori* limited in length by the vast amount of bridge material that has already been written.

If you incorporate all these tips into your game you will be well on your way to becoming a true expert, if you aren't one already. I hope that you have enjoyed my book and that it has been of some value to you. My overall message should be clear — always think for yourself about what you are doing and why you are doing it. Good luck and may your life overflow with masterpoints.

Recap

H ere is a recap of my main themes in the approximate order in which they appear:

TIPS 1-5

- There are five equally important dimensions of bridge: psychology, planning, technique, adaptability and judgment.

- The most effective table presence consists of relaxation and friendliness.

- Assess the skill level of your opponents and play accordingly.

- Notice all of your opponents' mannerisms and act on the basis of your observations.

- Be a good partner.

TIPS 6-15

- Stay alert; be ready when the declarer plays a card.

- Don't neglect to use deception; play so as to give the opponents the least chance of unmasking your ploy.

- Strive for a mere 85% success rate on saves and penalty doubles; anything higher means you are not being aggressive enough.

- Play your highest non-honor on the first trick when declarer leads trumps (in most situations).

- Don't obsess over errors or bad boards.

- Never be intimidated by reputation.

- Plan your plays; be flexible and modify them when indicated.

- Plan your entire bidding sequence before making your first bid.

- Don't try to make one bid do too much.

- Pay attention to details; watch the spots.

TIPS 16-25

- Count cards only when necessary.

- Count points whenever possible.

- Draw inferences from what partner and opponents don't do as well as from what they do.

- Be adaptable; experiment.

- Treat partner's signals as recommendations, not commands; you may know what to do better than he does.

- The five-level generally belongs to the opponents.

- Hands containing ten or more cards in two suits are powerful offensive hands, regardless of point count.

- When opening with 6-4 distribution, bid your four-card suit before rebidding your six-card suit if partner responds with a game-forcing bid.

- Go slowly with powerful defensive hands; avoid superaccepts that force you a level higher.

- Don't squander opportunities to penalize the opponents; recognize that artificial doubles (such as negative doubles) come with a cost.

- Don't sit for below-game penalty doubles if you have unmentioned trump support for partner.

- Corollary: in competitive auctions, strive to support partner at your earliest opportunity.

- Be liberal when it comes to opening 1NT.

- Patience is a virtue; you should often wait and gather additional information before bidding.

- It is safer to make a one-level overcall immediately after an opening bid than between two bidding opponents.

- Make marginal one-level overcalls only if they are essential for lead-directing purposes.

- Two-level non-jump overcalls require either an excellent suit or a powerful hand.

- Lead-directing doubles should focus on preventing partner from making his normal lead.

- Learn how to cuebid and use cuebids often.

- Avoid a jump to 4NT (if Blackwood); preserve the lower levels for cuebids.

- Your first cuebid shows extra values.

- Be sure both you and your partner know what the trump suit is before making any cuebids or using RKC Blackwood.

- Be imaginative — especially on opening lead.

- Against a suit contract, when holding K-x-x or longer in partner's bid suit, lead the king.

- Logic should always overrule rigid adherence to traditional principles.

- Don't signal unnecessarily.

- The best signaling convention is the one that conveys the most information with the fewest cards.

- Agree to play second highest from four small whenever partner needs to know if a ruff is available.

- A robust system taxes your memory; forgetting a convention carries a high price.

- Don't be a slave to your system; treat it as a framework, not a cage. Strive to make the best possible bid, even if it violates the requirements of a given convention.

TIPS 46-52

- Play puppet Stayman over 2NT openers.

- Don't make a positive response to a strong two-bid merely for the sake of showing two of the top three honors.

- Don't play support doubles or redoubles.

- Don't play systems-on when your 1NT opener is doubled for penalties.

- Don't play negative doubles when your partner opens 1NT.

- Don't play the 'principle' of fast arrival.

- Reserve a one-level double in the passout seat for an opening bid or better.

ABOUT THE AUTHOR

Dr. Romm received his B.Sc. degree at Caltech in 1962. He went on to attain an M.A. degree at UCLA where he also passed the Ph.D. qualifying exam in mathematics. He learned computer science at IBM as a systems analyst before entering a career as a manager of large computer projects at ARCO. After retiring at age 51, he received a J.D. degree from the University of Illinois law school. His hobbies are bridge, modern physics, philosophy and travel (having visited more than 70 countries). He has written *A Grain Of Salt: Why You Must Make Your Own Decisions* and is included in the 60th diamond edition of *Who's Who In America*. He is the father of two and currently resides in Seattle, WA.